TRAVELLERS

SOUTH AFRICA

By
MIKE CADMAN

Written by Mike Cadman
Updated by Robin Gauldie

Original photography by Mike Cadman and Trevor Samson

Editing and page layout by Cambridge Publishing Management Ltd,
Unit 2, Burr Elm Court, Caldecote CB23 7NU
Series Editor: Rosalind Munro

Published by Thomas Cook Publishing
A division of Thomas Cook Tour Operations Ltd
Company Registration No. 1450464 England

PO Box 227, The Thomas Cook Business Park,
Coningsby Road, Peterborough PE3 8SB, United Kingdom
E-mail: books@thomascook.com
www.thomascookpublishing.com
Tel: +44 (0)1733 416477

ISBN: 978-1-84157-804-0

Text © 2007 Thomas Cook Publishing
Maps © 2007 Thomas Cook Publishing
First edition © 2005 Thomas Cook Publishing
Second edition © 2007 Thomas Cook Publishing

Project Editor: Diane Ashmore
Production/DTP Editor: Steven Collins

All rights reserved. No part of this publication may be reproduced, stored in
a retrieval system or transmitted, in any form or by any means, electronic,
mechanical, recording or otherwise, in any part of the world, without prior
permission of the publisher. Requests for permission should be addressed
to Thomas Cook Publishing, PO Box 227, The Thomas Cook Business Park,
Coningsby Road, Peterborough PE3 8SB, United Kingdom.

Although every care has been taken in compiling this publication, and the
contents are believed to be correct at the time of printing, Thomas Cook Tour
Operations Ltd cannot accept any responsibility for errors or omissions,
however caused, or for changes in details given in the guidebook, or for the
consequences of any reliance on the information provided.

The opinions and assessments expressed in this book do not necessarily
represent those of Thomas Cook Tour Operations Ltd.

Printed and bound in Italy by: Printer Trento.

Front cover credits: Left © AWC Images/SIME-4Corners Images; centre
© Giovanni Simeone/SIME-4Corners Images; right © Giovanni Simeone/SIME-
4Corners Images
Back cover credits: Left © Damm Fridmar/SIME-4Corners Images; right
© Giovanni Simeone/SIME-4Corners Images

Contents

KEY TO MAPS

★   Start of tour

▲
2285m   Mountain

Introduction

Table Mountain stands tall over Cape Town with its fashionable beaches and productive winelands. Almost 2,000km (1,250 miles) to the northeast, the equally famous Kruger National Park shelters South Africa's largest population of elephants, lions and other creatures that thrive in the vast expanse of hot, wild bush. In between lies most of South Africa, a nation of more than 44 million people with a rich and complex social fabric, 11 official languages, a zest for sport, and a landscape that boasts remarkable geographic splendour and variety.

In KwaZulu-Natal, crystal-clear streams drain from the sometimes snow-capped uKhahlamba-Drakensberg mountains, while in the Northern Cape cheetahs and martial eagles search for prey in the rolling grass-covered sand dunes and desert scrub of the Kgalagadi Transfrontier Park. Along the country's west coast the icy Benguela current makes swimming a pastime only for the brave, but conversely Africa's southernmost coral reefs occur in the warm waters along the northeast coast.

The Durban beachfront, KwaZulu-Natal

These and other geographic and climatic contrasts contribute to making South Africa's flora and fauna amongst the most diverse of any region of comparable size anywhere.

In the middle of the country the teeming metropolis of Johannesburg and its neighbouring towns and cities attract visitors and work-seekers from all over the country, and even from neighbouring states.

South Africa is the economic powerhouse of Africa, and although many citizens are poor, the country has an extensive and well-maintained road system, efficient air links and good tourism infrastructure. The mining industry and rich deposits of gold, diamonds, platinum and other minerals have long been the mainstay of the economy. There is, however, an increasing focus on the technology, manufacturing and tourism sectors.

In some fields the constraints of apartheid are being shed relatively quickly, and today business leaders, politicians, academics and sportsmen and women come from all sectors of the country's diverse population. In other respects the transition from apartheid has not been as easy, but more and more children, known locally as the 'born frees', have no memory of South Africa without democracy, a concept which arrived with the 1994 election won by Nelson Mandela and his African National Congress party.

South Africa's youth, in keeping with global trends, are part of a rapidly urbanising population, and many people live in informal settlements around cities and towns.

South Africa's cities are not old by European standards – Cape Town, the country's oldest city, was open countryside in 1652, and Johannesburg is only 120 years old – but fossil evidence reveals an ancient history of human habitation. Some of the oldest hominid fossils on record have been found near Johannesburg, and archaeologists can trace fairly constant human habitation of the region for hundreds of thousands of years.

In recent history, migrants from many parts of Africa and Europe have made the country their home, and many South Africans' lives incorporate aspects of other cultures as a matter of daily routine. Cuisine, fashion and the arts all increasingly reflect this amalgam of traditions.

Introduction

Al fresco dining in Franschhoek, Western Cape

Geography and climate

South Africa covers some 1.2 million sq km (463,000sq miles) which is more than twice the size of France or a bit bigger than the US states of California and Texas combined. It lies roughly between 22 and 35 degrees south of the equator, and has 2,950km (1,830 miles) of coastline washed by the Atlantic Ocean in the west and the Indian Ocean in the east.

South Africa shares borders with Namibia, Botswana, Zimbabwe, Mozambique, Swaziland and Lesotho. The latter is entirely surrounded by South Africa.

The climate varies markedly, with most of the country experiencing the greater part of its rainfall in summer. On the Highveld (literally 'the high land'), and in the uKhahlamba-

CAPE TOWN
May–August
October–March

DURBAN
October–April
March–August

JOHANNESBURG
October–February
May–October

Drakensberg mountains, dramatic thunderstorms sweep across the countryside on summer afternoons often disappearing over the horizon and leaving clear rain-scrubbed skies.

The Western Cape has a Mediterranean climate and experiences warm-to-hot dry summers and cool, wet winters.

Temperatures in the interior sometimes climb to over 36°C (97°F) in summer, but in winter can plummet to well below 0°C (32°F) at night in the various mountain ranges and in the deserts. Deserts are not always hot, and although the Kalahari Desert regularly experiences daytime temperatures well over 40°C (104°F), night-time winter temperatures can drop as low as −10°C (14°F).

Most of South Africa lies on a plateau fringed by a coastal belt of varying width, and many of the basic geographic and climatic features spread across one or two, and in some cases several, provincial boundaries. The 2,300km (1,430 miles) Orange River for example, South Africa's longest river, rises in Lesotho and then flows along the borders of the Free State and Eastern Cape. It then heads through the Northern Cape to enter the Atlantic, where the borders of South Africa and Namibia meet.

A basic description of the geography and vegetation of each province is given on the following two pages. South Africa is comprised of nine provinces: Eastern Cape, Free State, Gauteng, KwaZulu-Natal, Limpopo, Mpumalanga, Northern Cape, North West and Western Cape.

Eastern Cape

Long, wide, sandy beaches characterise much of the Eastern Cape coast, although in the south, high forested ridges run right down to the sea providing spectacular views from cliffs above the waves. Further north the rugged Wild Coast, a region of sea

Jeffrey's Bay, a favourite surfing spot in the Eastern Cape

cliffs, deep river valleys and largely empty beaches begins. Not far inland, high fold mountains that sometimes receive snowfalls roll into the low scrub semi-deserts of the Karoo (*see Eastern Cape on pp38–43*).

Free State

The Free State is primarily open grassland, which begins to dissipate into the semi-deserts of the Karoo and Kalahari in the west. In the east, high ridges with sandstone cliffs form deep valleys, and in winter heavy snowfalls sometimes occur (*see Free State on pp44–5*).

Gauteng

Gauteng is generally a region of open grassland-covered plains ribbed with low ridges and the steeper Magaliesberg to the north. Much of the province is more than 1,500m (4,900ft) above sea level (*see Gauteng on pp48–61*).

KwaZulu-Natal (KZN)

The 3,200m (10,500ft) high uKhahlamba-Drakensberg mountains form the western boundary of this province. South Africa's highest point, Mafadi, 3,446m (11,300ft), is in the Injisuthi region of these mountains. The land falls away rapidly to the east in a jumble of rolling hills, which run down to the sub-tropical coast. The south coast has many rocky coves, but the beaches become sandier along the north coast (*see KwaZulu-Natal on pp62–83*).

Limpopo

Three major mountain ranges, the Waterberg, the Soutpansberg and the Northern Drakensberg cut through this province, which is primarily open *bushveld* (grassland savannah interspersed with thorn trees). The Drakensberg form the edge of the escarpment, which drops steeply to the Lowveld (low country). The Lowveld comprises many vegetation forms, but in simple terms is dominated by *bushveld* and *mopane* woodlands, which together cover much of the Kruger National Park. Summers are very hot and winters mild (*see Limpopo on pp84–5*).

Mpumalanga

High-altitude open grasslands in the west, south and south-east of this province drop to the Lowveld down northern Drakenberg passes similarly steep to those in Limpopo Province. This is an important farming province, and also includes the southern half of the Kruger National Park (*see Mpumalanga on pp86–95*).

North West

Much of this province is covered by open bushveld, and the Waterberg mountains act as an important watershed. In the centre of the province, the ancient Pilanesberg volcano makes a dramatic setting for the well-run Pilanesberg National Park. The west gives way to the arid Kalahari (*see North West on pp96–7*).

Northern Cape

The Northern Cape falls into the Karoo and Kalahari semi-desert zones. Much of the Karoo is covered with shrubs and sparse grasslands, and is an important cattle and sheep-farming region. Camel thorn trees, grasses specially adapted to the dry conditions and huge skies are the trademarks of the Kalahari. In the south-west the harsh Namaqualand region usually bursts into colour once a year as millions of flowers bloom after winter rains (*see Northern Cape on pp98–103*).

Western Cape

Although the west coast is cool and sparsely vegetated, the rest of this province's coastline is a mix of secluded coves, broad sandy beaches, and mountains that plunge directly into the ocean, breakers crashing at their feet. Inland, a maze of fold mountains finally gives way to the arid plains of the Karoo, the vast region extending over four provinces. Many of the famed Cape winelands shelter on the slopes and in the valleys formed by these mountains (*see Western Cape on pp106–21*).

Geography and climate

Hout Bay at night, Western Cape

History

100,000 BC Archaeological evidence shows southern Africa is already inhabited by *homo sapiens*.

8,000 BC San hunters inhabit parts of South Africa.

AD 1–1500 Iron-working spreads through central and southern Africa as Bantu people begin to move southwards and dominate the San and Khoikhoi peoples.

1488 Bartholomeu Dias rounds the Cape and reaches Mossel Bay.

1497 Vasco da Gama rounds the Cape and charts the sea route to India.

1652 Arrival of Jan van Riebeeck, first commander of the Dutch East India Company's Cape settlement.

1688 French Huguenots arrive.

1779 First of nine settler–Xhosa frontier wars in the Eastern Cape.

Slave bells, Stellenbosch

1795 First British occupation of the Cape.

1806 Second British occupation of the Cape.

1820 Large group of British settlers arrive in the Grahamstown area.

mid-1830s The Great Trek into the interior begins as Boers grow resentful of British rule in the Cape colony.

1838	Battle of Blood River: a small force of Voortrekkers defeats the Zulu.	**1950**	Various apartheid introduced and tightened during the next few years.
1850s	Independent Boer republics of Orange Free State and Transvaal are established.	**1952**	The ANC's defiance campaign begins.
1867	Discovery of diamonds near Kimberley – the diamond rush begins.	**1958**	Dr Hendrik Verwoerd becomes prime minister. Apartheid strictly enforced.
1879	Anglo-Zulu War: battles of Isandhlwana and Rorke's Drift.	**1960**	Referendum for South African independence. Sharpeville Massacre:

1880 First Anglo-Boer War (won by the Boers).

1886 Gold discovered. Johannesburg founded.

1899–1902 South African War (formerly the Anglo-Boer War – won by the British).

1910 Union of South Africa.

1912 The African National Congress is formed.

1913 The Natives Land Act reserves most land for the use of White people.

1948 Victory for the National Party in White elections.

Trinity Methodist Church, East London

demonstrators against the Pass Laws are fired on (69 killed, 180 injured). State bans ANC.

1961 South Africa leaves the Commonwealth and becomes a republic. The ANC begins its armed struggle. ANC leader Nkosi (Chief) Albert Luthuli wins Nobel Peace Prize.

1964 Rivonia Treason Trial: Nelson Mandela and seven other ANC members are sentenced to life imprisonment. South Africa excluded from Olympic Games.

A 19th-century carriage at the Calgary Transport Museum, Eastern Cape

1966 Verwoerd assassinated by parliamentary messenger.

1967 Professor Chris Barnard performs the world's first heart transplant.

1975 South Africa invades Angola.

1976 Police open fire on student protestors in Soweto on 16 June. The shootings lead to nationwide rioting, resulting in hundreds of deaths.

1977 Mandatory UN arms embargo. Steve Biko dies in detention.

1983 A new constitution allows three separate houses in parliament – for Whites, Coloureds and Indians.

1984 Archbishop Desmond Tutu wins the Nobel Peace Prize.

1985 ANC President Oliver Tambo, Rev. Jesse Jackson and Archbishop Huddleston head a 100,000-strong march through London demanding sanctions. State of Emergency declared in sections of the country. Political violence sweeps townships.

1985–86 Thousands of people are detained without trial during continued State of Emergency. Violence continues intermittently for next five years.

1989 F W de Klerk becomes president succeeding P W Botha.

1990 Nelson Mandela released from prison. The ANC and other banned political organisations are legalised. National Party government abandons apartheid, and begins negotiations to end it. The ANC suspends the armed struggle.

1992 Whites-only referendum leads to a 69 per cent vote to continue reforms.

1993 Nelson Mandela and President F W de Klerk share the Nobel Peace Prize.

1994 Democratic elections in April; ANC President Nelson Mandela elected President of South Africa. South Africa re-enters the Commonwealth.

1995 The Truth and Reconciliation

AIDS

The AIDS epidemic is one of the greatest issues facing South Africa, and has enormous social and economic consequences. Many children have been orphaned after their parents have died from AIDS-related diseases. Many skilled people have been lost to the economy after falling sick and later dying.

The Government was initially very slow to respond to the crisis and, in many cases, the private sector took the lead in education and medication.

Nearly all HIV in South Africa is spread through participating in unprotected sex. Blood transfusions in large hospitals are responsible for very few cases. Private hospitals use world-class technology.

Commission under Archbishop Desmond Tutu is appointed to hear evidence of apartheid atrocities.

1999 The second democratic election is held and Mandela steps down as President. The ANC wins and Thabo Mbeki becomes President.

2004 The third democratic election is held and the ANC returns to power. Mbeki remains President.

2009 Next elections due.

2010 South Africa to host FIFA soccer World Cup.

14

Politics

South Africa in the 21st century is a country hard at work creating an economically viable, functional democracy, but at the same time is intent on enjoying the journey. The excitement and sheer relief of the first-ever democratic election in 1994, the jubilation that greeted the election of Nelson Mandela as President and the realisation that South Africa could hold its head high in the global community of nations is old hat now. The memories of those heady days will always be treasured, however.

Now the euphoria has transformed into determination, and there is overwhelming consensus among citizens that there is an important task to accomplish. Alleviating poverty and unemployment and improving education and health are all major issues facing the government and the nation, but despite the scale of the task, there is no lack of enthusiasm. Most people accept that addressing these issues properly will be a major step towards helping to reduce the very high crime rate.

For much of the 1980s and early 1990s South Africa's political turmoil made international news headlines, and the name Nelson Mandela became famous all over the world. South Africa's transition to democracy without a full-blown war was hailed as an example of conciliation and common sense. The country has now had two fully democratic elections since 1994 and, although the ruling African National Congress (ANC) is by far the largest party, political debate and argument is vibrant and no more vituperative than in any other democracy.

Efforts are being made to provide better housing for dwellers in 'informal settlements' and townships such as Soweto and Cape Town's Cape Flats districts, but many feel the process is taking too long, and these deprived

Pretoria skyline

areas are a breeding ground for violent crime.

South Africa's next general election is due in 2009, and there are signs that the ANC will not win yet another landslide. The major opposition party, the Democratic Alliance (formed from the merger of the New National Party and the Democratic Party), may give the ANC stronger competition, while COSATU (Congress of South African Trade Unions), until now a loyal ANC ally, shows signs of developing into a working-class, left-wing opposition party in its own right.

Not all of the government's views, particularly with regard to the policies of some African countries' leaders and Middle Eastern politics, have met with the approval of developed nations. South Africa, nevertheless, maintains good relations with many countries around the globe. This level of international acceptance would have been unthinkable during the 1980s and early 1990s when apartheid was in its death throes.

During the 1980s, the National Party (NP) government clamped down hard on the popular uprising sweeping the Black townships, and tens of thousands of people, including children, were detained without trial. A series of States of Emergency were declared giving the police and military vast powers. For decades, many political books were banned – it was illegal to quote people like Mandela or even to possess his writings. Nearly all political opposition

A typical sign found throughout South Africa during the apartheid

was outlawed, and the press was severely censored. Thousands of people died in political conflict, many killed by police bullets. The political insurrection was the culmination of many events over many years. Apartheid was the formal policy of denying Black people the vote, the right to free movement, the right to employment and incorporated numerous other legalised injustices. Black people had been denied many rights since European settlers first arrived in Cape Town in 1652.

Resistance against discrimination manifested itself in many ways over the centuries. It was, however, only after the conservative National Party came to power in 1948 that parties such as the ANC began organised resistance in earnest. The 1960 Sharpeville Massacre, where police shot dead 69 protesters, and the life sentence handed down to Nelson Mandela in 1964 after he was found guilty of treason and sabotage, were just two of the incidents which raised the level of resistance. The state met this with severe oppression.

Thousands of people perceived by the state to be political opponents were jailed and many were tortured. In 1976 the Soweto riots, which were sparked after police opened fire on protesting school children, ignited nationwide unrest. This unrest continued sporadically until after Mandela was released from prison in 1990.

While the state was continually involved in attempting to suppress Black political aspirations, White South Africans enjoyed one of the highest standards of living in the world. This was at considerable cost, however, because international sanctions, sporting, cultural and travel restrictions eventually took their toll. To exacerbate matters, the aggressive NP leadership drew South Africa deeper and deeper into guerrilla wars in neighbouring states, first in Namibia (South West Africa), over which they had been given control by the League of Nations in 1919, and later in Angola.

By the mid-1980s economic sanctions had tightened considerably and this, coupled with the expense of fighting wars in neighbouring states, had a serious impact on the economy. As the Berlin Wall was coming down and many former Soviet States were undergoing their own liberation, the South African government buckled under both internal and international pressure. The government finally made the decision to release Mandela and un-ban political parties.

In 1990 Mandela walked free, and four years later, after prolonged and intense negotiations by representatives of nearly all South Africans, he ushered in a new South Africa to the salute of military helicopters flying the country's new flag and the acclaim of a rapturous nation.

Statue of Cecil John Rhodes in Cape Town

Mounted police patrol past the Houses of Parliament in Cape Town

Culture

South Africa's cultural heritage reflects the country's complex history, and African, European and Asian influences all thread their way through the art, music and literature of the region. South Africa's relatively recent transition to democracy has led to a significant shift towards exploring and embracing Africa's rich cultural background, and this heritage is actively being promoted with a greater sense of pride than at any other time in history.

Art

South Africa's oldest art form (*see panel on p22*) is the rock art and engravings of the San (Bushmen). However, the 17th, 18th and 19th centuries saw the development of a school of European artists intent on creating a record of the landscapes, people and animals in what was to them a strange new country.

Perhaps the best known of these painters were Thomas Baines and Thomas Bowler whose work created an accurate, if somewhat stylised, record of the country as it then was.

African beadwork at a flea market

Music

Whether the music is played on a cowhide drum, a *marimba* (a form of xylophone usually made from a gourd), a Stradivarius violin or an electric guitar, someone in South Africa will consider the entertainment 'traditional'. As with so many other aspects of the country, local music has its roots in many cultures and traditions, and is continually evolving according to new demands and trends. Western and African influences mix easily, and radio stations and music stores offer everything from *kwaito* (a form of rap), reggae, jazz, blues, classical and hard rock to general pop. Jazz trumpeter Hugh Masekela and singer Miriam Makeba have been known internationally since the 1960s, and younger artists such as Yvonne Chaka Chaka with her cross-cultural rhythms have built followings across Africa. The piano work of Abdullah Ibrahim (formerly Dollar Brand) has reached almost cult status in some quarters.

Johnny Clegg and his bands Juluka and Savuka pioneered a mix of traditional Zulu music and modern soft rock, and the Soweto String Quartet have managed to combine a mix of classical, jazz and African music into a huge popular product. Music is important to many South Africans, and the focal point of many a tavern or restaurant is the radio or hi-fi.

In rural areas homemade instruments are common, and they are often ingeniously created from items designed

New African art by Thabo Nyelele

Western influence continued to dominate until well into the 20th century, but artists such as Walter Battiss slowly gave painting a more South African flavour.

Black artists including George Pemba and Gerard Sekoto, although almost unknown in South Africa at the time, took this trend to a new level in the 1940s, and today their work fetches high prices. Later in the 20th century, many artists began using their work as a form of protest against apartheid. Modern South African art draws on many influences, and increasing numbers of young South Africans are focusing on more traditional African styles. Many art galleries and markets also sell traditional African day-to-day items including bowls, sleeping-mats and symbolic beadwork as art.

PIERNEEF MUSEUM

The Pierneef Museum, Graaff Reinet, Eastern Cape

for anything but making music. Lengths of fishing line, seeds from trees and disused motor-oil cans are adapted for use in guitars, rattles and drums.

Architecture

South African architecture is a bewildering mix of old, new, rural and modernist, with a huge dose of practicality thrown in for good measure. Older cities are a mix of glass and steel modernist structures, dull and conservative 1960s office blocks and the occasional Art Deco or Victorian building.

Sandton, near Johannesburg, has been developed over the past 25 years, and is the largest conglomeration of new buildings in the country, with an unusual mix of avant-garde constructions, pseudo-European plazas and even buildings ostentatiously decorated with Roman-style pillars and facades.

Many of the Victorian buildings are found in Pietermaritzburg, Durban and Cape Town, but many smaller towns such as Oudtshoorn contain good examples of this style, a legacy of British colonisation. Perhaps the most well-known form of South African architecture is the Cape Dutch style, prevalent from the early 18th until the mid-19th century. This is best displayed in Cape Town itself and the nearby winemaking towns of Stellenbosch, Franschhoek, Paarl and Tulbagh. Thatched-roof buildings with decorative rounded gables and white walls preside over rows of vines. Most have large, ornate double doors and square windows with carefully tended wooden frames.

The ornate Union Buildings in Pretoria – built by Sir Herbert Baker in 1912 – are, arguably, the most easily recognised architectural landmarks in the country. Decorated with stone pillars and friezes, they are still used as the seat of government.

Residential architecture ranges from the opulent – built in whatever style the owner can afford – to the tiny, almost square 'matchbox' houses built as housing for Black people in the formerly racially segregated townships. In poor informal settlements, shacks are often made of corrugated-iron sheeting, wooden-crate panels and even plastic – they may not qualify as architectural masterpieces, but they are home to millions of people. In rural areas, traditional Xhosa, Zulu or Venda huts are still used, but many have been adapted over the years. Zulu 'beehive' huts were made with grass thatched over a wooden frame, although traditional Xhosa and Venda homes tended to have mud walls.

Literature

Although most South African literature is written in English or Afrikaans, the country's writers have explored a wide range of themes and social issues, and their works largely trace the development of modern South Africa. Many writers have achieved

Traditional singers on the Victoria & Alfred Waterfront, Cape Town

Culture

international recognition, and the Nobel Prize for Literature was awarded to two South Africans in recent years. Nadine Gordimer (1991) and J M Coetzee (2003), although very different in style, both examine the psychology of apartheid and post-apartheid South Africa. The theme has been consistent among many writers, and the classics *Cry, the Beloved Country* by Alan Paton (1948), *Down Second Avenue* by Es'kia Mphahlele (1959) and *Country of my Skull* by Antjie Krog (1998) dig deeply into the country's collective psyche.

South African poetry covers a very broad range of subjects, ranging from the South African War (Anglo-Boer War), through to a celebration of nature, love and the freedom struggle. Poets, including Sipho Sepamala and Mafika Gwala, used their work to try to raise political awareness when other forms of political expression were outlawed. South Africa has also produced many writers of popular fiction – Wilbur Smith is one of the best-selling authors of all time. Although not literature in the classic sense, South Africa has a very strong publishing industry based on the environment and wildlife. A huge variety of high-quality coffee table books, field guides and popular science works are available at good bookstores.

Drama

Many South African playwrights and actors have achieved international fame. Athol Fugard and John Kani have received critical acclaim in New York, London and elsewhere.

The performing arts have a strong base and long tradition in South Africa and perhaps reached their peak in the last years of apartheid when theatre gave voice to protest that would otherwise have been silenced.

The Market Theatre complex in Johannesburg and others risked closure by running some political performances. Today that courage has been transformed into a desire to teach, and many theatres run courses helping train aspiring actors.

Every year in June, Grahamstown in the Eastern Cape runs a week-long arts festival (*see Eastern Cape section, pp38–43*) where both established and fringe actors, playwrights and other performers strut their stuff. Various smaller festivals are hosted elsewhere in the country (*see pp24–5*).

ART

Perhaps some of the most unusual art galleries in the country are the rock overhangs and shelters where San (Bushmen) artists used vegetable and animal blood paints to record hunting, ceremonies and other scenes.

The San wandered through South Africa as long as 40,000 years ago, and left one of the largest collections of rock art in the world scattered throughout the more mountainous areas of South Africa.

Their paintings and rock engraving tell stories of their daily life, but they also had spiritual significance. The richest collections are found in the uKhahlamba-Drakensberg mountains in the Eastern Cape and KwaZulu-Natal.

African Footprint, a big, bold African musical, was a huge success and even played in China.

Various symphony orchestras perform regularly, and some of the larger cities host ballets and opera, often with international guest artists performing. In poor areas, many churches and other groups run choirs which give public performances, helping to create pride and status for people who struggle to make a living.

Culture

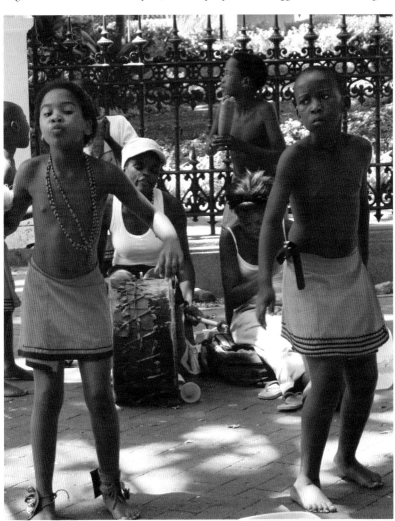

Children dancing in Company's Gardens, Cape Town

Festivals

Most festivals in South Africa are modern events and few have the ancient traditions of those in Europe, Asia or South America. This does not detract from the fun though, and many festivals, and some sporting events, are a good excuse for a party, something South Africans find hard to resist.

Not all festivals are held annually, and it is a good idea to check with tourism authorities about events planned in each region.

January
Cape Town New Year Carnival
Thousands of singing, dancing minstrels move through the streets of Cape Town. Everyone parties.

February
Dias Festival
Mossel Bay. Food and cultural festival.

March
Klein Karoo National Arts Festival
Afrikaans cultural festival with theatre, music and other entertainment in Oudtshoorn.

The North Sea Jazz Festival, Cape Town

Cape Town Festival
Art, music and other events.

April
Rand Show
A huge consumer show with everything from cars and computers to candyfloss. Held in Johannesburg.
North Sea Jazz Festival
Cape Town. Two days of world-class jazz. Billed as 'Africa's Grandest Event'.
Port Elizabeth's Splash Festival
Water sport, music and other events.

May
Sabie Forest Fair
Mpumalanga. Various events.

June
Paternoster Seafood Festival
Western Cape. Lots of fresh seafood, wine and music.

July
National Arts Festival
Grahamstown. The biggest event of its

kind in South Africa. Theatre, music and other entertainment.

Knysna Oyster Festival

Knysna. Road-running marathons, bicycle races, oysters and other food. The town is usually packed.

August

Winter Witblits Festival

Prince Albert. *Witblits* is powerful home-brewed alcohol, but the festival is also about food and fun.

September

Hello Darling Arts Festival

Darling, Western Cape.

Hermanus Whale Festival

Hermanus. Coincides with peak whale-viewing times. Lots of events.

October

Stellenbosch Food and Wine Festival

Stellenbosch.

Tulbagh Festival

Tulbagh, Western Cape. Various events.

Jacaranda Festival

Pretoria. Various events.

November

Cherry Festival

Ficksburg, Free State. To celebrate the cherry harvest.

December

Knysna Street Carnival

Holiday crowds having fun.

Spier Summer Arts Festival

Runs until March. Concerts and other entertainment.

Minstrels entertaiin the crowds at the Cape Town New Year Carnival

Wildlife

The bio-diversity of southern Africa is extraordinarily varied. Although it only comprises around one per cent of the Earth's landmass, the region hosts more than 340 mammal species, which is about eight per cent of the worldwide total. South Africa also hosts about 880 bird species, and more than one quarter of all living land tortoise species. Altogether more than 400 species of reptile occur in southern Africa – by comparison around 300 species are found in the whole of mainland United States of America.

South Africa's biological diversity is due to the wide variety of habitats that occur in the region. They range from the *fynbos* (a group of plants of which 67 per cent occur only in South Africa) of the western and southern Cape, to sub-tropical coastal forest in KwaZulu-Natal, grasslands in the central regions and savannah in the north and northwest.

Additionally, two ocean currents flow along South Africa's coastline influencing both marine and terrestrial life. The warm sub-tropical Agulhas Current surges down the east coast, while the cold, nutrient-rich Benguela nourishes sealife and influences weather patterns along the west coast.

Game reserves are sprinkled across the country, each with its own treasures and attractions. South Africa

Female elephants are very protective towards their young

is one of the easiest places in Africa to see 'The Big Five': elephant; lion; rhino (both black and white); leopard and buffalo.

Although these, and predators including the cheetah and wild dog, are considered to be the glamour species, many antelope and smaller species are no less interesting and deserving of attention. The very common impala, zebra, giraffe, wildebeest, baboons, warthogs and dozens of other species all fill important ecological niches and provide endless photo opportunities.

In case these creatures do not provide adequate entertainment, South Africa has many even less well-known animals. Who would not be delighted to spot a pygmy hairy-footed gerbil, a tiny 25g (one-ounce) rodent that lives in the western parts of South Africa, or even the short-snouted elephant shrew that lives in the hot, dry northern parts of the country?

Birds also range from the large and spectacular to the tiny and unobtrusive. The large eagles and vultures usually occur in game reserves and remote areas where food is plentiful. Lappet-faced and Cape vultures, both with wingspans of over 2.5m (8ft), martial, bateleur and black-breasted snake eagles excite even experienced birders. Less dramatic are hundreds of other

species including the colourful lesser double-collared sunbird and the unobtrusive fairy flycatcher, which tips the scales at just over 8g (little more than a third of an ounce).

Also at the diminutive end of the scale is the world's smallest tortoise, the speckled padloper, which measures just 10cm (almost 4in) across its carapace. This tortoise, which occurs only in the Western Cape, is threatened both by habitat loss and the pet trade.

Whales and dolphins are plentiful in South African waters, and in season are easily and often seen from the shore (*see whale-watching feature on pp122–3*).

A large number of excellent guidebooks covering mammals, birds, reptiles, trees and other subjects are available in South African book shops (*see directory on p142*).

The fastest land mammal, the cheetah, can reach a speed of 100kph (62mph)

Some common animals of the bush

Although spotting the 'Big Five' is the highlight of a visit to the bush, there are many other animals, which are no less interesting and will almost certainly be seen more often.

They all play an important role in the jigsaw puzzle of ecosystems – remove one species entirely and it affects the whole picture.

Cheetah

With its long legs and lithe body the cheetah is clearly built for speed – a design which has made it the fastest mammal on earth. Cheetahs (*see below*) hunt small antelope, and

sometimes prey as small as rabbits, by slowly stalking them and then bursting into an explosive sprint. They tire quickly and not every hunt is successful. Cheetahs are the slightest of the large cats, with males weighing up to 60kg (132lb), and are often robbed of their kills by spotted hyaenas, leopards and, sometimes, lions.

Giraffe

Besides their obvious size and height – males weigh up to 1,200kg (2,640lb) and stand 5m (16ft 5in) tall – giraffe,

when seen up close, have wonderfully long eyelashes. Nobody is sure why this is so, but it might be to protect their eyes when browsing on thorn trees.

They are common in many of the game reserves, particularly in the northern and eastern parts of the country.

Impala

The graceful impala is one of the most common animals in the Kruger National Park and many other game reserves. Many people simply drive past them because they are so common, but it's well worth spending time watching them.

Most lambs are born in November, and a couple of months later can be seen gathered together in nursery groups within the herd. Only males have horns.

Kudu

The tall, handsome kudu is the most common of all the large antelope and sometimes lives quite close to farmhouses and other human habitation. The males have beautiful long, spiralled horns. Kudu usually live in small herds.

Springbok

South Africa's national animal prefers the drier central and western regions of the country. They used to form herds hundreds of thousands strong as they followed the rains, which generate fresh grazing. Today their population is much smaller, but springbok are common enough in game reserves and on many farms.

Gemsbok

Long, rapier-like horns are the most obvious feature of this large, powerful antelope. It too is a creature of the drier areas and happily survives in the middle of the Kalahari Desert. They

do not need to drink water for most of the year, deriving all their moisture requirements from their food. Gemsbok also have very sophisticated body-cooling systems and water utilisation abilities.

Spotted hyaena

These powerful predators have had a bad press and are not in any way as cowardly as they are so often portrayed in popular stories and movies. They often hunt for themselves and can bring down prey as large as a wildebeest weighing over 200kg (440lb).

Nevertheless, they are very effective scavengers too, and use their immensely powerful jaws to tear skin and crack bone that not even lions can handle.

Steenbok

These tiny antelope are common in many parts of South Africa. Many are often seen in the same area because they form territories which they defend against other steenbok. They only weigh about 11kg (24lb).

Impressions

South Africa is an easy country to visit. All the major centres are linked by regular flights, the road system is good, and there are excellent hotels, B&Bs, game reserves and national parks. All the major centres have a wide range of well-stocked shops, medical care is first class and the telephone system and internet facilities are the best in Africa. The tourism industry has grown by leaps and bounds in recent years and service standards are good.

Climate

Cape Town and the southern Cape coast have a Mediterranean climate with warm-to-hot summers and mild-to-cool winters, which is when most of the rainfall occurs. Elsewhere in South Africa, most rainfall occurs in summer.

The Victoria & Alfred Waterfront, Cape Town

In many parts of the interior of the country it can become very hot in summer, particularly in the Kruger National Park, Kgalagadi Transfrontier Park and parts of KwaZulu-Natal. Winter days in the interior are cool, but at night the temperature can fall below freezing. The coastal belt of KwaZulu-Natal is very humid in summer.

School holidays

Most South Africans take their annual holidays over Christmas or Easter, and more popular destinations are accordingly very busy. Although the crowds create an exciting atmosphere, tourists with some flexibility in their schedule might want to avoid these peak periods.

What to take

All the major cities are well stocked with almost any item of clothing or equipment the average traveller might need – so should anything be forgotten there is no need to panic.

Health

Good medical care and hospitals are available throughout South Africa (*see box on AIDS on p13*). Consult your doctor or a travel clinic about anti-malaria medication if you intend visiting the hot northern and northeastern parts of the country, particularly the Kruger National Park and the game reserves of northern KwaZulu-Natal. All tap water is drinkable. Use sunscreen, even in winter, as South Africa has very high rates of ultra-violet radiation.

Access for disabled persons

Although some buildings and public areas have been made user-friendly to disabled people, this is not widespread. Larger airports have been designed or adapted to assist disabled people.

Getting around

• All the larger centres are linked by air, and cars are easily hired at airports.

• Public transport is not good, and in smaller centres or rural areas taxi services are poor.

• It is best to make transport arrangements at the hotel or B&B and to take advantage of local knowledge.

• Avoid the ubiquitous minibus taxis, unless you are prepared to endure bad driving and poorly maintained vehicles.

• Several reputable companies operate long-distance coaches between major centres, but be aware that distances can be intimidating. Cape Town, for example, is 1,500km (930 miles) from Johannesburg.

• There are tolls on some major roads. Cash or credit cards are accepted.

• South Africa has an extensive rail system linking all the major centres. The luxurious Blue Train runs between Cape Town and Johannesburg, and is an easy way of seeing some of the countryside in comfort.

The Tsitsikamma mountains on the Garden Route

Self-drive

It is a good idea to carry a mobile phone in case of a breakdown or some other emergency. Programme important numbers like that of the car rental company, the Automobile Association and your hotel into the phone so you can find help easily should you experience a breakdown.

South Africans are, as a rule, poor drivers so exercise caution on the roads. Should the driver of the minibus taxi travelling in front of you activate the hazard lights on his vehicle, it means he is about to stop, whether it is legal or not, to collect or drop off passengers. Be alert. (On major routes drivers sometimes use their emergency flashers as a means of thanking you for allowing them to pass.)

Urban myth says that, because of the crime rate, people may feel unsafe and it is therefore acceptable to stop at red traffic lights late at night, and then continue on your way if the road is clear. It is not acceptable, and it is illegal. Wait for the green.

Crime

This subject is always at the top of most people's list of concerns. Yes, South Africa does have an abnormally high crime rate, but the best protection against criminals is common sense. Tens of millions of South Africans use this tactic on a daily basis.

Take sensible precautions as you would anywhere else in the world, and, if in doubt, ask your hotel, B&B or tour guide for advice.

• If you are ever in the unfortunate position of having someone armed with a weapon attempting to steal your car or anything else, never ever resist. The situation is unlikely to arise but, if it does, let the thieves take whatever they want.

• Don't carry unnecessary cash or valuables, and do not leave cameras or bags on the seat of your car. Store them out of sight, preferably in the boot. Lock your doors.

• It is best to take tours to some areas rather than drive yourself. Again, ask advice. Avoid self-appointed 'guides' who approach you in the street.

While it is important to be alert,

Transport takes many forms in South Africa

Impressions

remember the vast majority of tourists never experience crime so don't let the subject dominate your holiday.

Visiting game reserves and dealing with wildlife

Never feed wild animals, whether in game reserves or not, because the animals begin to associate humans with food. This later causes conflict with humans, and authorities end up having to shoot problem animals that are a threat. Human food also creates health problems in wild animals.

• Baboons and monkeys are particularly good at begging, extremely clever, strong, very fast and take advantage of humans in a flash. No matter how cute they look, do not feed them.

• Don't get out of the car in Big Five game reserves as some species are potentially dangerous.

• If you encounter elephants while driving in a game reserve, always give them space to move off, and do not get between adults and babies. They are usually accustomed to cars and pose no threat, but it is best to give them space.

• If you have been walking through long grass, check your legs and arms for ticks afterwards. Several anti-tick sprays are available.

• Most mosquitoes start biting in the evening, so it is a good idea to wear long trousers and long sleeves if you want to avoid getting bitten. Use mosquito repellents too.

Monkeys at Kruger Park

Language

South Africa has 11 official languages, and a list of useful phrases in all 11 would take up half this book.

English is widely spoken, and nearly all signage is in English. Other languages, including Afrikaans, Zulu and Xhosa, sometimes appear on signboards.

For the record, the 11 languages are English, Afrikaans, Ndebele, Northern Sotho (Pedi), Siswati, Southern Sotho, Tsonga, Tswana, Venda, Xhosa and Zulu.

Etiquette

South Africans are generally friendly and welcoming towards tourists. Most people are willing to offer advice and suggestions and are happy to chat with foreigners about sport, politics or whatever subject seems appropriate.

A friendly 'Hi, how are you?' will elicit an acknowledgement and probably the same question in response which forms a good platform for any conversation.

When meeting people, a handshake is a widely accepted form of greeting. Some Black people use a more complicated handshake, which involves the standard grip, and then, without releasing, slipping your hand around the other person's thumb, then returning to the traditional grasp.

Money

Travellers' cheques are accepted in most banks, and credit cards are used throughout the country. Credit cards are not accepted for fuel. Most banks issue a separate card for fuel purchases.

Clothing

The South African lifestyle is fairly casual. In summer, many people wear shorts, casual shirts, and sandals, particularly at the coast and in game reserves. For those unused to harsh sunlight, it is wise to remember to use sunscreen on legs and arms when wearing shorts and T-shirts. Dress in good restaurants is slightly more formal, but jackets and ties are unnecessary unless on business.

Before you leave

Visit the South African Tourism website to catch up on links to the latest shows,

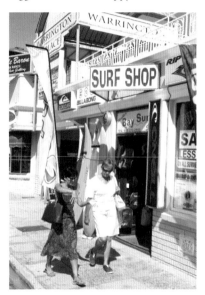
The popular seaside town of Hermanus

big sporting matches and other events that will add to the enjoyment of your trip.

South Africa Tourism
Tel: 0870 155 0044.
www.SouthAfrica.net

Quiet and peaceful Swellendam is one of the oldest towns in South Africa

Townships

Visitors to South Africa are often confused by the reference to 'townships' rather than suburbs or cities. Although Soweto is a huge area with a population of millions, it is usually referred to as a 'township in Johannesburg' but is in reality part of the same conurbation. The same rule applies to Kwa-Mashu near Durban, Zwide near Port Elizabeth and Mamelodi near Pretoria.

As with many things in South Africa, townships came about as a result of the apartheid policy of separate development – segregating people on the grounds of race – and were created as residential areas

Fruit seller in Soweto

exclusively for Black people. Black people were only allowed into the formerly 'White' cities to provide labour, and apartheid planners decided that housing and other facilities were to be kept at the most basic level possible. Most houses were tiny, almost square 'matchbox' houses with no electricity and no running water inside the houses. Toilets were built outside and used a night soil system where tankers collected buckets of sewage a few times a week. Initially, most roads were unpaved and street lighting was non-existent.

In terms of the policies of 'separate development', Black people needed a permit to be in White urban areas, and White people needed special permission from the authorities to visit townships. Neither permit was easy to obtain and applications were often denied. Even today many White South Africans have never visited a township despite working or playing sport with people who have lived there all their lives. Most townships were originally built with few access roads to make it easy for police to monitor comings and goings. Because the townships were intended as labour dormitories, almost no formal commercial

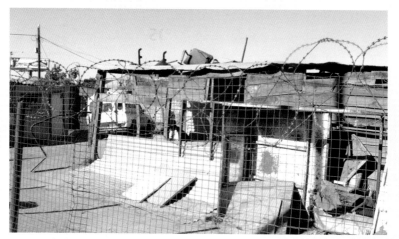

Soweto is the largest township in South Africa and parts of it are still very impoverished

developments such as supermarkets were allowed, forcing Black people to shop 'in town' – usually the nearest city.

Today townships are changing daily with increasing numbers of urban people having access to electricity, telephones and running water, and most roads are now tarred. Some of the informal settlements that have sprung up in and near townships still lack even these basics.

It may seem odd to treat townships as tourist attractions because, quite obviously, they are not galleries or museums. The experience is, however, well worth the time because Gugulethu is a vastly different place to the suburbs of Cape Town, as are the streets of Mamelodi and Pretoria. Every city has several townships, usually hidden out of the way, and even small towns have their own 'townships'.

They are usually lively, friendly places where everyone seems to know everyone else, a characteristic often lacking in the some of the formerly 'Whites-only' suburbs in many South African cities. Kids yell as they play soccer in the streets, and enterprising mechanics and welders repair cars at the street side while customers wait. Noisy *shebeens* (formerly illegal bars but still called *shebeens* even though they are now legal) are scattered along busy roads. People socialise easily and, on Sunday, many people dressed in their best outfits chat in the streets while walking to church. A tour to a township is an essential, entertaining and educational trip and should not be missed.

www.gauteng.net

Eastern Cape

Eastern Cape locals are often quietly smug that 'their' broad beaches, numerous mountain ranges and historical sites are seldom deluged with the crowds that Cape Town or Durban sometimes receive. The residents and tourism authorities here are only too happy to welcome tourists, but they are quick to point out that their province is a good place to 'get away from it all'. The climate is mild and ideal for holidays all year round. www.ecapetourism.co.za

Port Elizabeth

Although a fairly sedate provincial city, Port Elizabeth is well placed to make the most of good but quiet beaches and interesting history-rich countryside. The city also makes a good base from which to visit the Addo Elephant National Park and the scenic Baviaanskloof Wilderness Area.

The area saw the first meetings, and clashes, between Khoikhoi, British, Dutch, German and Xhosa people. The 1820 settlers from Britain landed here, and there are still many well-preserved buildings from the era throughout the region.

Nelson Mandela Bay Tourism
Tel: (041) 581 7540.
www.ibhayi.com

The Nelson Mandela Metropolitan Art Museum (formerly King George VI Art Museum and Gallery)

The museum houses various exhibitions from the Eastern Cape and elsewhere in South Africa, as well as international art, including Chinese textiles and Indian miniature figurines.
1 Park Dr, Port Elizabeth 6001.
Tel: (041) 586 1030.
www.artmuseum.co.za.
Closed for renovations until July 2007.

Grahamstown's cathedral dominates the skyline

No 7 Castle Hill Museum

This museum is housed in one of the oldest settler cottages in Port Elizabeth. The cottage was built in 1827 and has been restored to its original state. Various displays reflect the lifestyle of the 1820 settlers.

7 Castle Hill, Central. Tel: (041) 582 2515. Open: Mon–Fri 10am–4.30pm. Admission charge.

Bayworld Complex

Dolphins, fossils and reptiles are all features of this complex, which unsurprisingly incorporates a museum, dolphinarium and snake park.

The museum exhibits a wide range of natural and cultural history displays, and the dolphinarium presents daily shows. Nearby the snake park has an impressive range of residents.

Humewood. Tel: (041) 584 0650. www.bayworld.co.za. Open: Mon–Sun 9am–4.40pm. Call to confirm times of dolphin shows.

Grahamstown

Today Grahamstown is a small university town, but in the early 18th century it was a turbulent frontier post where European settlers clashed regularly with the Xhosa over land and cattle.

The cathedral is the focal point of the town which has many old buildings that have been restored to their original condition. Several museums explain both social and natural history. The South African Institute for Aquatic Diversity is the most unusual, and contains one of the most comprehensive exhibits of aquatic life ever collected.

During university term, students throng the streets of the town and give pubs and restaurants a lively, cheerful atmosphere. Between 27 June and 6 July the town hosts South Africa's largest arts and theatre festival, which attracts thousands of visitors.

Grahamstown Tourism

63 High St. Tel: (046) 622 3241. www.grahamstown.co.za

National Arts Festival

Tel: (046) 622 7115. Call to confirm dates and bookings. www.nafest.co.za

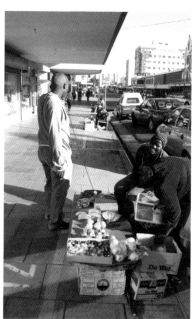

Informal traders in East London

Elephants in Addo National Park

1820s Settlers' National Monument and Memorial Museum

Houses a collection of artefacts from the time, ranging from toys to weapons.
Somerset St. Tel: (046) 622 2312.
Open: Tue–Fri 9.30am–1pm & 2–5pm,
Sat 9am–1pm.
Admission charge.

South African Institute for Aquatic Biodiversity

Somerset Ave.
Tel: (046) 636 1002.
www.nrf.ac.za.
Open: Mon–Fri 8am–5pm.
Admission charge.

Addo Elephant National Park

Originally created in 1931 to protect the last 11 elephants found in the region, this reserve now has a healthy population of over 450 elephants. This is the largest elephant population south of those in the Kruger National Park and KwaZulu-Natal. The thick vegetation also supports black rhino, antelope and other smaller creatures.
Addo is about 70km (45 miles) northwest of Port Elizabeth.

National Parks Board Central Reservations

Tel: (012) 428 9111.
www.sanparks.org.
Open all year.

East London, Port Alfred and King William's Town

Wide, open beaches and pleasant farming land make this region popular as a family holiday destination. There are many good swimming beaches, hiking trails and nature reserves.

King William's Town is a former frontier outpost where the Xhosa and Khoikhoi people often clashed with settlers. The excellent Amathole Museum has a collection of exhibits of 19th-century life and Xhosa culture, as well as a large collection of South African mammals. Huberta, a hippo that walked more than 1,000km (629 miles) down the South African coast in the late 1920s and early 1930s, is preserved here. (Nobody knows why she walked that far.) The East London Museum contains the world's only dodo egg and also has a preserved specimen of a coelacanth (*see panel on p43*).

East London Museum

Entrance in Dawson St.
Tel: (043) 743 0686.
Open: Mon–Fri 9.30am–5pm, Sat

*2pm–5pm, Sun & public holidays
11am–4pm.
Closed: Christmas Day & Good Friday.
Small admission charge.*

Anne Bryant Art Gallery
*Upper Oxford St.
Tel: (043) 722 4044.
Open: Mon–Fri 9am–5pm, Sat & public
holidays 9am–12pm. Closed: Christmas
Day & New Year's Day.
Admission charge.*

East London City Hall

Calgary Transport Museum
*13km (8 miles) from East London on
N6 to Stutterheim.
Tel: (043) 730 7244.
Open: daily 9am–4pm.
Closed: Good Friday & Christmas Day.
Small admission charge.*

Amathole Museum
*Albert St, King William's Town.
Tel: (043) 642 4506.
Open: Mon–Sat 9am–4.30pm,
Sun 10am–3pm.
Admission charge.*

Gately House
*1 Park Gates Rd. Tel: (043) 722 2141.
Open: Tue–Thur 10am–1pm &
2pm–5pm, Fri 10am–1pm, Sat & Sun
3pm–5pm.
Admission by donation.*

Wild Coast
This remote coastline of sea cliffs, broad
lagoons and open countryside runs from
just north of East London all the way to
KwaZulu-Natal. A variety of hotels and
smaller lodges are dotted all the way
along the coast, which is still relatively
undeveloped and would suit people
looking for a quiet beach holiday away
from the main tourism beat.

This area is also the graveyard of
many ships, wrecked by the powerful
currents and heavy seas that sometimes
occur along this coast.

Wild Coast Tourism
*Tel: (043) 722 2203.
www.wildcoast.org.za*

Amatola Mountains and Hogsback

These mountains, some 200km (125 miles) north of Port Elizabeth and 120km (75 miles) northwest of East London, are one of South Africa's better-kept secrets. Many parts of the range are grasslands, and there are extensive forests which are ideal for hiking, climbing, mountain biking and fly-fishing.

The region is rich in Xhosa culture, and the nearby University of Fort Hare houses an important collection of African art. The village of Hogsback is quaintly reminiscent of England, and makes a good base to explore the region. There are no fewer than 23 waterfalls in the area.

Hogsback Tourism Bureau
Tel: (045) 962 1340.

A B&B in the lush Hogsback region

Mountain Zebra National Park

This park was originally established to save the Cape mountain zebra from extinction. It has succeeded in that goal to the point that some animals have been relocated to repopulate other Karoo parks.

Nature trails and walks cross the 6,536-hectare (16,150-acre) reserve, and a good variety of wildlife including kudu, springbok and birds occur.

Booking through SA National Parks Central Reservations
Tel: (012) 428 9111.
Open: all year round.

Graaff Reinet

Many of Graaff Reinet's historic flat-roofed Karoo cottages, Cape Dutch and Victorian buildings have been colourfully restored. The town makes an eye-catching contrast to the semi-desert scrub that covers the mountains around the town.

The Grootkerk (large church) is a copy of Salisbury Cathedral in England, and the Drostdy Hotel has been restored to its 1806 grandeur. More than 200 buildings in the town have been declared national monuments. The Old Library houses a large collection of fossils, and Reinet House, which is claimed to have the world's largest living grape vine in the garden, is a museum with displays explaining the region's history. The town was founded in 1786.

Graaff Reinet Publicity Association
Tel: (049) 892 4248.

The Owl House, Nieu-Bethesda

J H Pierneef Museum
Tel: (049) 892 6107.
Open: Mon–Fri 8am–5pm, Sat & Sun
9am–noon. Admission charge.

Reinet House
Tel: (049) 892 3801.
Opening times as above.
www.graaffreinet.com
Admission charge.

Close to Graaff Reinet
About 55km (34 miles) north of Graaff
Reinet (close in Karoo terms) is Nieu-
Bethesda village where the Owl House
is a monument to the reclusive sculptor
Helen Martins (1898–1976). Hundreds
of her sculptures of owls, animals and
people fill the garden, while the house
is a dream world of murals, mirrors
and eerie lighting (*www.owlhouse.co.za*).

Other artists have since moved to the
remote town to enjoy the peace and
inspiration of the Sneeuberg mountains
and wide-open spaces of the Karoo.

Ibis Art Centre
Nieu-Bethesda.
Tel: (049) 641 1623. (The centre doubles
as the tourism bureau.)

The Karoo Nature Reserve
Some 16km (10 miles) outside Graaff
Reinet, the Valley of Desolation offers
fantastic views across the plains and
mountain ranges of the Karoo. The
region is rich in fossils, a legacy of the
period more than 300 million years ago
when marshes and moist forests
covered the landscape.

Graaff Reinet Publicity Association
Tel: (049) 892 4248.

Coelacanth display, East London Museum

THE COELACANTH

In 1938 the modern world's first coelacanth
(*Latimeria chalumnae*) was caught off the
East London coast. Previously it had only
been known from fossil remains, although in
recent years scientists and fishermen have
caught more specimens. It is a fish with fins
that resemble primitive stump-like legs –
hence ichthyologists affectionately referring to
the fish as 'old four legs'.

Free State

The Free State is a quiet agricultural province where everything moves along at a sedate rural pace. Even the citizens of the capital city Bloemfontein don't pay too much attention to the world rushing by – they're too happy enjoying the nearby wide open spaces and blue skies. Most tourists head for the mountainous south-east, but there are rewarding cultural sites, museums and other attractions all over the province.

Clarens

The wide-open grasslands and maize fields of the central Free State give way to mountains and sandstone bluffs near the pretty village of Clarens close to the Lesotho border.

The town has become an artists' haven, and dozens of galleries have sprung up in the town, which is rapidly becoming a favourite weekend haunt. The Easter weekend is the busiest of the year.

The clear, cold streams and mountain air make for good biking, horse riding, hiking and trout fishing.

Clarens Publicity Association
Tel: (058) 256 1542.
www.clarenstourism.co.za

Golden Gate National Park

Set in amongst sandstone mountains with crystal-clear streams and dams, the park offers excellent walking, hiking and horse riding. San hunters used to shelter here, and a variety of grassland game species still occur. Winters can be cold with snowfalls.

The park is very close to Clarens and it is worth visiting both areas during the same trip. The nearby Qwaqwa Mountain Park is undeveloped but offers good mountain scenery. There is a Basotho cultural village, which depicts traditional life.

South African National Parks' Central Reservations
Tel: (012) 428 9111.
Nearby are the QwaQwa National Park and the Sterkfontein Dam Nature Reserve.

A mural in Clarens, Free State

Bloemfontein

In Afrikaaans, Bloemfontein means 'flower spring', and in Sotho the area was known as Manguang, 'the place of leopards'. Today the town has grown into the largest city in the Free State.

There are several museums and monuments, but the most significant is the National Women's Monument and War Museum commemorating the 26,000 Boer women and children who died in British concentration camps during the South African War of 1899–1902. An estimated 14,000 Black people accused of being Boer sympathisers died in separate camps.

Bloemfontein Publicity Association
Tel: (051) 405 8489.
www.bloemfontein.co.za
(Site being upgraded.)

National Museum

Corner Charles St and Aliwal St.
Tel: (051) 447 9609.
Mon–Fri 8am–5pm, Sat 10am–5pm,
Sun noon–5pm. Admission charge.

Freshford House

31 Kellner St. Tel: (051) 447 9609.
Mon–Fri 10am–1pm, Sat 2pm–5pm.
Admission charge.

National Women's War Memorial and War Museum

Monument Rd. Tel: (051) 447 3447.
Open: Mon–Fri 10am–5pm, Sat
8am–4.30pm, Sun 2pm–5pm.
Admission charge.

Sandstone bluffs dominate the scenery of the eastern Free State

THE GREAT TREK

In 1835, two groups of Dutch-speaking Boers left the Cape for the unknown interior in the Great Trek. They felt that the colonial government had failed to provide protection against the Xhosa in the never-ending battle for land, while the abolition of slavery had robbed them of valued possessions.

One group of Voortrekkers, led by Piet Retief, went into Zululand where Dingane massacred their advance party. Revenge was the horrible Battle of Blood River, followed by the establishment of the Republic of Natalia (1838), which Britain annexed. The Boers then trekked north and, in 1860, founded the South African Republic (ZAR). The other party of Voortrekkers trekked beyond the Vaal and Orange rivers and proclaimed the Orange Free State (1854).

Train journeys

South Africa is one of the few remaining countries where you can still experience magical railway journeys in trains of enormous prestige. Make an epic journey conjuring up the romance of a lost age of steam travel, or take a short trip for just a day out or a weekend away.

Under steam
The epic journey
Rovos Rail

The magnificently restored, privately owned Pride of Africa, travels a variety of routes. From Cape Town, destinations include Victoria Falls (Zimbabwe) and Dar es Salaam (Tanzania), with stopovers at Matjiesfontein, Kimberley and Pretoria, and optional sightseeing en route.

Sleepers, dining car and observation carriages are the refurbished originals, a reminder of pre-war opulence.
Tel: (012) 315 8242.
www.rovos.co.za

Shongololo Express

Named after a local millipede, this service offers luxurious train rides taking in all the highlights of South Africa from the Kruger National Park to Cape Town. The trains also travel to eight other southern African countries. Choose from three 8-day and three 16-day tours.
Shongololo Express
Tel: (011) 781 4616.
www.shongololo.com

Union Limited

A steam locomotive and original carriages of the old Union Limited, the first luxury train (1923) taking first-class passengers from Johannesburg to Cape Town to meet the ocean liners, have been transformed into a 'safari' train with a variety of routes and destinations.
Transnet
Tel: (011) 773 9523.
www.transnetheritagefoundation.co.za

Short excursions
Banana Express

The Banana Express steams its way from Port Shepstone through coastal hills and sugar-cane fields to the Oribi Gorge Nature Reserve. The round trip takes a few hours and makes a good day out.
Tel: (039) 682 4821. Call to confirm schedule.

Magaliesberg Express

The South African National Railway and Steam Museum Preservation

Group offers day trips from Johannesburg Station to the Magaliesberg (see p60).
First Sunday of every month from Johannesburg's Park Station.
Magaliesberg Tourism
Tel: (012) 888 1154.
www.magaliesberg.co.za.
Call to confirm schedule.

Die Herrie
Operating between Oudtshoorn and Calitzdorp, the train traverses ostrich country and the Karoo.
Tel: (044) 272 2377.
Call to confirm schedule.

Outeniqua Choo-Tjoe
This distinguished old steam train covers the George to Knysna section of the Garden Route (see Garden Route feature on pp134–7), and is probably one of the country's most enjoyable services, passing through spectacular scenery.
Tel: (044) 801 8228.
Mon–Sat, but call to confirm schedule.
4–6 hour round trip.

The Apple Express
The Apple Express runs from Port Elizabeth, and crosses the historic Van Staden's river bridge, the highest narrow-gauge railway bridge in the world.
Tel: (041) 583 2030.
www.appleexpress.co.za

Diesel or electric train travel
The Blue Train
The Blue Train replaced the old Johannesburg-Cape Town Union Limited train in 1939. Its name derives from the colour of the original train.

Today's Blue Train is one of the great trains of the world, a slower alternative to flying (Cape Town–Pretoria, 24 hours), but an infinitely superior experience. It has sleeping accommodation with showers, a dining and lounge car, and space to carry cars.

An additional newer Transvaal Lowveld Route, Pretoria to Nelspruit, is an excellent springboard for visits to the Kruger National Park. There are also trips to Victoria Falls in Zimbabwe.
Tel: (021) 334 8459.
www.bluetrain.co.za

Regular passenger services
Regular inter-city trains traverse some amazing landscapes. The best routes are the Trans-Karoo, the Trans-Orange, the Trans-KZN and the Algoa Express. There are a variety of discounts for children and senior citizens.
Transnet
Tel: Toll free (086) 000 8888.
If calling from outside South Africa.
Tel: (012) 315 2757.

Gauteng

Almost 120 years ago, the world's richest gold deposits were discovered near what is today Johannesburg. Prospectors, speculators and the merely hopeful flocked from across the globe to the sweeping grasslands and ridges of the South African Highveld in search of quick success and, sadly for most, elusive fortunes. Today, the concrete, steel and glass office towers and efficient infrastructure of Johannesburg, its glitzy sister city Sandton and nearby Pretoria act as similar symbols of hope, offering jobs and opportunity to people from all over southern Africa.

Gauteng is the economic heartland of South Africa and, although it is the country's smallest province, it generates more than a third of the nation's gross domestic product (GDP).

The region is home to some of the most powerful mining companies in the world, and boasts the largest

Office blocks dominate the skyline of wealthy Sandton

concentration of technology, financial services and manufacturing expertise in Africa.

Gauteng has a long history of human habitation, and archaeologists have unearthed some of the world's oldest hominid fossils dating back some 3.3 million years at several sites – most notably at the Sterkfontein Caves, 45 minutes north of central Johannesburg.

The climate is comfortable, with warm summers and cool, clear winters, although the region's high altitude – it is on average about 1,600m (5,200ft) above sea level – sometimes results in icy nights.

JOHANNESBURG AND SANDTON

Johannesburg and its satellite city Sandton are the symbols of the upwardly mobile in South Africa. A widespread perception is that everything happens faster, and that everything is bigger and better than

Nelson Mandela Square in Sandton

elsewhere. This belief is reflected in the expensive cars, big houses, fashionable shops and upmarket restaurants. But the region is also one of many contrasts. Just as the stores in Sandton carry famous clothing labels and jewellery brands, shops in the nearby dormitory areas of Soweto and Alexandra stock only basic foods and other household essentials.

A tour to Soweto or Alexandra provides an important insight into the development of South Africa, and also offers a glimpse of energetic, largely cheerful township life.

Downtown Johannesburg bustles with traders and shoppers from throughout the region. Colourful fabrics decorate storefronts, and informal chefs roast *mealies* (corn) on street corners. Hundreds of minibus

taxis piled high with goods leave crowded ranks to ferry people around the metropolis, to rural areas and to countries as far away as Zimbabwe and Zambia.

An evening spent at the Market Theatre or a club in the Newtown Precinct will confirm the cultural diversity of the city, as will a visit to the sidewalk cafés in Melville. The fashion-conscious hang out in Nelson Mandela Square or Rivonia Road, or visit the antique shops and cafés of Parkhurst on weekend afternoons.

Surprisingly for such a large, densely populated city, there are many nature reserves. At the Walter Sisulu Botanical Gardens (formerly the Witwatersrand National Botanical Gardens), carefully tended displays of plants from all over South Africa thrive, while on the cliffs above the rolling lawns a pair of wild black eagles continue to breed, as they have done for more than a decade.

Apartheid Museum

A plethora of multimedia displays take the visitor through the stark cruelty of racial separation enforced by apartheid, but also showcase South Africa's remarkable transition to democracy. The story of political and social upheavals is skilfully told, and provides an invaluable insight into the development of modern South Africa.
Gold Reef Road, Crown Mines.
Tel: (011) 309 4700.
www.apartheidmuseum.org.
Open: 10am–5pm. Closed: Mon, Good Friday & Christmas Day.
Admission charge.

Apartheid Museum, Johannesburg

Constitution Hill

South Africa's new Constitutional Court has been built here around the notorious former prison called The Fort. Many famous prisoners, including Nelson Mandela and Mahatma Gandhi, were once held in the prison. Various parts of the prison are used as galleries explaining the history of The Fort.
Constitution Hill, Braamfontein.

Gauteng Tourism
Tel: (011) 327 2000. www.gauteng.net
Open: daily 9am–5pm.

Gold Reef City

The theme park has been built around an authentic 19th-century gold mine. Visitors can travel 200m (650ft) underground down a mine to learn about the industry and the history of South Africa's biggest gold rush. Buildings from the period have been restored around the Number 14 Shaft of the original Crown Mines. Various other forms of entertainment are offered, including 'gumboot dancing' made famous by migrant workers in the mines. There are amusement park rides and a hotel and casino nearby.
Crown Mines. Tel: (011) 248 6800.
www.goldreefcity.co.za.
Open: Tue–Sun 9.30am–5pm.
Closed: Mon.
Admission charge.

Johannesburg Art Gallery

This large gallery has one of the country's best art collections. Works include those by local and international

THE LIBERATION STRUGGLE

Although it was formed in 1912, the ANC only resorted to taking up arms after it was banned by the state in 1960. Initially most military actions took place in the form of sabotage of power lines and other infrastructures. In the 1970s and 1980s, however, armed guerrillas sometimes clashed with security forces and made bomb attacks against both strategic and civilian targets.

As the nationwide civil unrest of the 1980s intensified, ANC supporters also clashed with those of the Inkatha Freedom Party and others perceived to be supporters of the state. Troops and riot police patrolled the townships almost constantly from 1984 and clashed with ANC supporting youths on a daily basis. This violence continued until the early 1990s, even after Mandela was released.

artists, both contemporary and classical. Gerard Sekoto, Sydney Kumalo and Alexis Preller are well represented, and there are works by Claude Monet, Edgar Degas and other artists. There are many collections of local beadwork, carving and other exhibits.
Joubert Park. Tel: (011) 725 3130.
It is best to visit with a tour guide
as the Joubert Park area is unsafe
for tourists.

Markets

Over 500 stalls at the **Rosebank Mall Rooftop Market** offer crafts, arts, books, clothing and food. The market is particularly good for African carvings, masks, figurines and jewellery. Food is available too.
Open: Sun 9am–4pm.

The Bruma Fleamarket offers a wide variety of goods, including African artwork, carvings and other curios. As with the markets listed above, bargaining is acceptable and expected. There are food stalls, and on weekends and holidays there is entertainment too, often in the form of traditional dancers.
Corner Marcia Ave and Ernest
Oppenheimer St, Bruma.
Tel: (011) 786 0776.
Open: daily 9am–4pm.

The **Mai Mai Market** specialises in traditional medicines used for both physical and spiritual health. The majority of Black people in South Africa consult both western-style and traditional doctors, and many African products are available here. Most stallholders will happily explain the

Zulu trader in the Mai Mai Market, Johannesburg

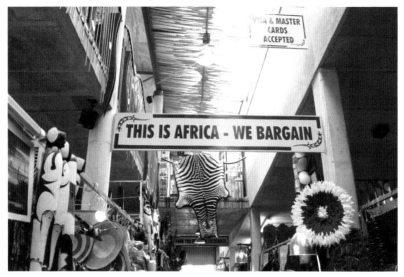

African Craft Market in Rosebank

myriad uses of plants and animal parts. The stalls are not for the squeamish, because of the many animal bones, skins and horns on display, but they are an integral part of African culture. *Corner of Anderson St and Berea St, Johannesburg.* *Open: Mon–Sat all day. Closed: Sun. Hard to find, and in a run-down area, so taking a guide is advisable.*

MuseuMAfricA

This is Johannesburg's major cultural history museum and is housed in the old Market Building which was built in 1913. Permanent exhibitions include displays of South African rock art, geology, and photography dating back 100 years.

The dangers of mining and the rise of township jazz are among several

themes highlighted. The 'Tried for Treason' display tells the story of Nelson Mandela and 155 other prisoners who went on trial in 1956 for their anti-apartheid activities. *121 Bree St, Newtown.* *Tel: (011) 833 5624.* *Open: 9am–4pm. Closed: Mon, Good Friday, Christmas Day & Day of Goodwill.* *Small admission charge.*

Sandton

Sandton City, Nelson Mandela Square (formerly Sandton Square) and the nearby Hyde Park Corner Shopping Centre form the heart of the wealthy shopping areas of the lush northern suburbs. African fashion and influences rub shoulders with imports directly from Europe. The season's trends and famous labels are all important to well-heeled shoppers browsing the boutiques.

A range of upmarket coffee shops and cafés provide useful vantage points to watch who is buying what, and good bookstores and cinemas offer somewhat more cerebral relaxation.

Sandton City

5th St, Sandton.
Tel: (011) 883 2011.
Open: daily from 8am.

Nelson Mandela Square

5th St, Sandton.
Tel: (011) 784 2750.
Open: daily from 8am.

Hyde Park Corner Shopping Centre

Jan Smuts Ave. Tel: (011) 325 4340.
Open: daily from 8am.

South African Lipizzaners

These powerful white 'dancing horses' are famed for their skill in executing complex movements in the classical traditions invented by Spanish riding masters during the Middle Ages. The Kyalami Centre is the only riding school outside of the Spanish Riding School in Vienna, Austria, with official approval to conduct Lipizzaner performances.

There are 65 of these rare horses based at Kyalami, and every Sunday expert riders put the stallions through their complex routines.

1 Dahlia Rd, Kyalami.
Tel: (011) 702 2103.
www.lipizzaners.co.za.
Shows: Sun 10.30am.
Admission charge.

Shopping at Sandton City, Sandton

THE SOUTH AFRICAN WAR

Following success in the First Anglo-Boer War (1880), the Transvaal Republic regained independence from Britain. By then its gold was attracting droves of foreign prospectors. British imperialists instigated the Jameson Raid (1895), hoping to ignite an uprising followed by the installation of a British administration. Its failure and ensuing events led to the South African War (1899).

President Kruger's commandos defeated the British at Talana Hill and routed them at Nicholson's Nek, but their siege of Ladysmith proved to be disastrous and ultimately cost them the war. By 1900, Pretoria had surrendered. A rural guerrilla war resulted in savage retribution: Boer women and children were imprisoned in the world's first concentration camps. The horror of these led ultimately to the Peace of Vereeniging (1902).

South African National Museum of Military History

This museum contains a unique collection of weaponry and uniforms spanning 120 years of South African military history, including the Anglo-Zulu War, the South African War, the First and Second World Wars and the liberation wars fought during the birth of modern South Africa.

The displays include artillery pieces, tanks and other armoured vehicles, a German-made, two-man mini-submarine and the only preserved World War II Messerschmitt Me 260 B jet night fighter.

Herman Ekstein Park (close to the Johannesburg Zoo), entrance intersection Erlswold and Eastwold Avenue, Saxonwold. Tel: (011) 646 5513. www.militarymuseum.co.za. Open: daily 9.30am–4.30pm. Admission charge.

Soweto

The vibrant dusty streets of Soweto provide a fascinating insight into the complex world of South African society. Built by apartheid's planners merely to provide labour for industry, Soweto and other townships have a life and culture of their own, and are a world apart from the western orientation of Johannesburg's more affluent areas.

Much of the struggle against apartheid took place in areas like Soweto, and there are several memorials to those who died, including the Hector Peterson Memorial in Orlando West.

Most tours take in these memorials as well as the former homes of two Nobel Peace Prize winners, Nelson Mandela and Archbishop Desmond Tutu. Both homes are in Vilakazi Street, the only street in the world that can boast two Nobel Prize winners.

The sprawling township of Soweto

Elsewhere, visitors get a flavour of township life visiting small restaurants or *shebeens* (bars).
Taking an organised tour is advised, and several operators run tours to Soweto, Alexandra and other townships.
Gauteng Tourism
Rosebank Mall.
Tel: (011) 390 3614.
www.gauteng.net

Walter Sisulu National Botanical Gardens

Formerly the Witwatersrand National Botanical Gardens, this 300-hectare (740-acre) area features a variety of walks through the landscaped and natural *veld* areas, which showcase many species of indigenous plants. Over 230 species of birds have been recorded as well as a number of small

Walter Sisulu National Botanical Gardens, near Johannesburg

REGINA MUNDI CHURCH

Regina Mundi, sometimes known as 'The Queen of Soweto', is a church that has played a pivotal role in the township's turbulent political history.

During the apartheid years, the huge Catholic Church, which can seat 2,000 people, was often used as a venue for political gatherings, many of which were disrupted by police using tear gas and, in some instances, guns. During the 1976 Soweto uprisings, children wounded by police gunfire took refuge in the church, as did many others in later years.

Today the church, built in 1964, has had a park created in its gardens, and inside the church there is an art gallery featuring the history of Soweto and Johannesburg.

mammals. The 70m- (230ft-) high Witpoortjie Falls is visible from most parts of the gardens, which also include a small dam and bird hide.

Open-air concerts are held in winter, when the sun is still warm but rain is unlikely, and many bring picnics and sit on the rolling lawns while listening to the music.
Malcom Road, Poortview, Roodepoort.
Tel: (011) 958 1750 or 958 0529.
www.nbi.ac.za.
Open: 8am–5pm all year.
Admission charge.

PRETORIA

Pretoria is South Africa's capital but, despite its political importance, this small city moves at a relatively leisurely pace. The city has been the seat of various South African governments for most of the last 110 years beginning with the Boer Republics, which declared independence from Britain in the late 1800s, and most recently the African National Congress-controlled government.

As the home of the country's civil service and international diplomatic corps, it is a fairly staid city, although vibrant pockets of restaurants and clubs keep students and more adventurous officials up until the early hours. The University of Pretoria is one of South Africa's largest, and is known for its wildlife and, in particular, mammal research, and the nearby Transvaal Museum has important collections of a wide range of species.

Various museums and art galleries reflect much of South Africa's past, but also illustrate the constantly developing nature of the country's social and political structure. At the start of the hot summers, much of the city becomes covered in the purple blossom of the jacaranda trees that line many of the wide streets.

Melrose House

Set in verdant gardens, this museum was originally a Victorian home built in 1886. Later it became the headquarters of the British forces fighting against the Boers in the South African War of 1899–1902.

Throughout the latter years of the war, generals briefed Queen Victoria from the house, and in 1902 the Treaty of Vereeniging was signed here, ending the conflict.

The architecture of the house and displays of furniture and other *bric-a-brac* provide a good example of the tastes of wealthy Victorian colonial settlers. Displays of period

Union Buildings

photographs reveal the harsh conditions of this war.

Snacks are served in the gardens.
275 Jacob Maré Street, Pretoria.
Tel: (012) 322 0240.
Open: Tue–Sun 10am–5pm.
Admission charge.

Pretoria Art Museum

This important museum has fine examples of many forms of South African art, including contemporary work as well as those of older, more established artists.

South Africa's best-known 'old school' painters such as Anton van Wouw, Maggie Loubser, Henk Pierneef and Irma Stern are exhibited, and many prints and other media from the 18th and 19th centuries are also displayed. The gallery highlights the transition of modern South African art away from a purely eurocentric base, and also emphasises the use of more unorthodox media.
218 Vermeulen Street.
Tel: (012) 344 1807.
www.pretoriaartmuseum.co.za.
Open: Tue–Sat 10am–5pm, Sun 12am–5pm. Closed: Mon &
public holidays.
Small admission charge.

The Union Buildings

Designed by the famous British colonial architect Sir Herbert Baker, and completed in 1913, the Union Buildings have loomed large in the minds of South Africans ever since.

For a long time the seat of the apartheid government, these sandstone buildings represented to many the oppression of apartheid rule. In 1994, it was here that Nelson Mandela was sworn in as president.

Perched on a hill, the buildings and surrounding gardens provide good views of the city.
Tours of the gardens can be arranged
Mon–Fri. Contact local tour operators
(see Directory on pp187–8).

Transvaal Museum

This museum has one of the best collections of southern African birds, mammals, insects and reptiles in the country.

The displays provide a complete overview of nearly all the species most people are likely to see. A wide range

Transvaal Museum

of lectures and presentations are offered throughout the year, and special programmes for children are also presented.

It is a working museum, and research staff contribute significantly to the knowledge pool of many species on a regular basis.

Paul Kruger Street, Pretoria.
Tel: (012) 322 7632.
www.nfi.co.za.
Open: Mon–Sat 9am–5pm, Sun 11am–5pm. Closed Christmas Day & Good Friday.

Voortrekker Monument

Just outside Pretoria the huge granite Voortrekker Monument is visible for kilometres, and commemorates the spirit of the Voortrekkers who left the Cape in 1834. The monument also depicts a belief that God supported them in their various battles.
Open: daily 9am–4.30pm.
Admission charge.

FURTHER AFIELD IN GAUTENG

Chameleon Market and Informal Market

A huge range of African arts and crafts are available from both the formal and informal markets here. Weekends are busy as there are many tourists and locals on their way to Sun City, or just enjoying a day in the sun shopping for bargains. Traders come from as far afield as Kenya, Senegal and the Democratic Republic of the Congo, and

some of the goods on sale reflect their origins.

The market is at the foot of Commando Nek, near the Hartebeespoort Dam wall. It is 25 minutes from Pretoria and about 50 minutes from Johannesburg. It is a good place to stop while on the way to Sun City or the Pilanesberg National Park.

Cradle of Humankind

The area of rocky grass- and shrub-covered hills and valleys some 45 minutes north of central Johannesburg has proven to be one of the most important hominid fossil sites in the world.

Already more than 500 hominid fossils and 9,000 stone tools have been uncovered, including an almost complete 2.6 million-year-old *Australopithecine* skull fondly known as 'Mrs Ples'.

There are 12 distinct sites scattered along the Sterkfontein Valley, including the Sterkfontein Cave, Wonder Caves and Swartkrans where there is evidence of the earliest known deliberate use of fire about 1.3 million years ago.

African fabrics

Market near Hartebeespoort Dam

Various operators run tours to The Cradle and there is an excellent restaurant nearby.

Maropeng Visitor Centre
Off R400 highway.
Tel: (014) 577 9000.
www.maropeng.co.za

Sterkfontein Caves Visitor Centre
Tel: (011) 668 3200
www.maropeng.co.za.
Admission charge.

Crocodile Ramble

This area borders on the Magaliesberg region, and there are dozens of art galleries, craft shops, cafés and hotels. Many people from both Johannesburg and Pretoria spend a Saturday or Sunday wandering around various parts of the Ramble area shopping or having tea or lunch. Contact the Ramble tourism office for an electronic or print brochure. Events and exhibitions change regularly. The area

also borders on the Cradle of Humankind (*see p58*).
Tel: (014) 577 9323.
www.crocodileramble.co.za

Cullinan

The largest diamond ever found, the whopping 3,106-carat Cullinan diamond, was found here in 1905. Still a rich source of diamonds, the mine

CASINOS

Although a relatively new phenomenon in South Africa (because they were outlawed prior to 1994), casinos are hugely popular, and the spinning wheels and bright lights attract thousands of hopeful customers daily.

The casinos and accompanying hotels tend to be situated near the larger cities, but operate in all of the nine provinces. Some of the larger casinos are part of large shopping complexes or have other attractions, including amusement parks, nearby.

South Africa also has a national lottery. It is known as The Lotto, for which winners are selected every Wednesday and Saturday.

offers regular tours where the mining process – from digging the first hole to cutting the final gem – is explained.

The village has many well-preserved homes and buildings and various museums stores and quiet restaurants help complete a morning or afternoon visit. The village is about 60km (37 miles) east of Pretoria.

Cullinan Tourism
Tel: (012) 734 0081.
Mine tours: Mon–Fri.

Lesedi Cultural Village
Xhosa, Zulu, Pedi and Basutho homesteads have been built within the village where visitors experience something of the many traditional cultures that make up South Africa. Guides explain some of the intricacies of each culture, and audiovisual displays are also used.

Dancers later entertain tourists while lunch is served. A variety of curios and artwork is available as is overnight accommodation.

Hartebeespoort Dam

Call management for directions. About 45 minutes from Johannesburg and 25 minutes from Pretoria.
Tel: (012) 205 1394.
www.lesedi.com.
Tours: daily 11.30am and 4.30pm.
Admission charge.

Magaliesberg Mountains
Many residents of nearby Pretoria and Johannesburg escape the cities on weekends to enjoy outdoor pursuits in the rolling countryside near the high southerly facing cliffs of the Magaliesberg mountains, which run for some 100km (60 miles) east of Pretoria.

Many B&Bs and country lodges are scattered throughout the region, and innumerable stalls and shops offer crafts, country food and other paraphernalia.

Horse riding, hiking, camping and bird watching are just some of the outdoor attractions which attract day-trippers, although others simply visit the area for a quiet weekend lunch and a bit of casual shopping. The Magaliesberg are easily accessible from both Johannesburg and Pretoria.

Magaliesberg Tourism
Tel: (012) 888 1154.
www.magaliesberg.co.za

Suikerbosrand Nature Reserve
High grass-covered hills and rocky stream valleys give visitors an idea of what the area around Johannesburg would have looked like before the city developed.

A surprising amount of small game including antelope occurs in the 13,337-hectare (32,950-acre) reserve, which is near the town of Heidelberg some 45km (28 miles) from the centre of Johannesburg. Hiking trails, a circular drive and picnic sites can be found here.

Johannesburg and the surrounding urban sprawl are visible from the northern side of the reserve and provide a sobering reminder of how much humans have changed our planet.
Tel: (011) 904 3930.
Open: all year.

Soapstone elephant

KwaZulu-Natal

The 3,000m- (9,840ft-) high, sometimes snow-covered peaks of the uKhahlamba-Drakensberg mountains in KwaZulu-Natal slope steeply to sub-tropical, banana-tree-fringed beaches less than 200km (125 miles) to the east. Further north along the hot and humid coastline, Africa's southernmost coral reefs shelter a plethora of brightly coloured fish and other sealife. While only a few kilometres inland, the Big Five thrill tourists in some of Africa's oldest game reserves.

The North Coast, South Coast and Durban area itself offer good surfing, safe bathing and many exciting dive sites. Between the mountains and beaches, the rolling hills and grasslands of the Midlands and surrounding areas provide some of the best agricultural land in South Africa.

The geographical diversity of KwaZulu-Natal is matched by the cultural mix of its residents. Zulu, British and Indian traditions combine to create a vibrant mosaic of cuisine, dress and culture.

KwaZulu-Natal, formerly known simply as Natal, was colonised by the British in the 19th century. The province later saw several wars fought between the settlers and the Zulu, and later the Boers (of Dutch descent).

Late in the 19th century, labourers were brought from India to work in the sugar-cane fields. Today, the province has the largest Indian community in the country. Zulu people make up the majority of the population and,

accordingly, their influence in local government and culture is significant.

Many Zulu people live in rural areas and follow a traditional way of life but often move easily between city and country life.

DURBAN

Warm seas, broad beaches and easy access to the province's many attractions make Durban one of South Africa's most important holiday destinations. Over Christmas, the beaches are packed with holidaymakers, but the city's sub-tropical climate encourages tourists at any time of the year. In the middle of what passes for winter, the city hosts one of the world's top surfing events. Winter daytime temperatures seldom fall below 21°C (70°F), and summer highs often exceed 30°C (86°F).

Culturally, Durban is a vibrant mix of African, Western and Indian cultures. Churches, mosques and synagogues rub shoulders with street

Durban City Hall

stalls where traditional doctors sell medicines to cure ailments or to ward off evil spirits. As befitting a city with a large Indian population, Durban has become famous in South Africa as the home of hot, spicy curry dishes, but a cosmopolitan range of restaurants provides fare suitable for most palates. Shopping opportunities are nothing if not eclectic, and stores selling the latest electronic goods can be found next to noisy bazaars selling everything from shovels to chicken food.

African Art Centre

Telephone-wire *imbenge* (baskets), beaded wooden or clay animals, ceramics, carvings and other items are made by Zulu and Xhosa women. It is well worth booking a lecture with one or more of the artists who will explain the cultural significance of beadwork and other items.
Tourist Junction, 160 Pine St.
Tel: (031) 312 3804. www.afri-art.org.za.
Open: Mon–Fri 8.30am–5pm, Sat 9am–1pm.

Coedmore Castle and Kenneth Stainbank Nature Reserve

Coedmore Castle was built by the Stainbank family in 1885 and today contains many of the original household contents which provide an interesting insight into colonial life. The castle is in the Kenneth Stainbank Nature Reserve, which protects an important remnant of the coastal forest that once covered much of the region.

A visit to the reserve shows what parts of Durban would have looked like 200 years ago. More than 300 species of birds and a relatively large number of mammals have been recorded here. Visitors can combine a visit to the castle with tea and a walk in the reserve. Many people pack a picnic to enjoy amongst the forest trees.

Coedmore Castle
Yellowwood Park. Tel: (031) 462 3005.
Call to book a visit. Admission charge.

Kenneth Stainbank Nature Reserve
Yellowwood Park. Tel: (031) 469 2807.
Open: 6am–6pm in summer,
6.30am–5.30pm in winter.
Small admission charge.

Durban City Hall, Durban Art Gallery and Natural Science Museum and Kwazuzukwazi Science Centre

The City Hall complex hosts civic functions and occasional symphony concerts. It also houses the Durban Art Gallery and Natural Science Museum. The Art Gallery has several important displays including a comprehensive collection of Zulu beadwork, while the Natural Science Museum has good displays of animals and birds. Nearby, the Local History Museum and the Old House Museum explain Durban's colonial history. The City Hall was built in 1910, and is unusual in that it is a replica of the Belfast City Hall in Northern Ireland.

City Hall & Durban Art Gallery
Smith St. Tel: (031) 311 2264.

Open: Mon–Sat 8.30am–5pm, Sun &
public holidays 11am–5pm.
Natural Science Museum
Tel: (031) 311 2256. Same opening times
as City Hall.
Old House Museum
31 St Andrews St. Tel: (031) 311 2261.
Open: Mon–Sat 8.30am–4pm, Sun &
public holidays 11am–4pm.

Killie Campbell Museum

Set on the Berea Ridge overlooking the
city, this museum is housed in
Victorian-era Muckelneuk Mansion,
the former home of sugar baron Sir
Marshall Campbell. There is an
extensive library of Africana books,
manuscripts and maps.

It also contains an important
collection of Zulu art, as well as

displays of musical instruments,
pottery, weapons and other items.
The Berea also provides excellent
views of Durban.
220 Marriott Rd, Berea.
Tel: (031) 207 3432.
Viewing by appointment: Mon–Fri
8.30am–4.30pm.

Mosques and Hindu temples

Durban has a rich variety of Muslim
mosques and Hindu temples, and
several have been declared national
monuments. The Juma Mosque is the
largest Muslim place of worship in
South Africa, and is a well-known
landmark. Its golden domes and ornate
architecture form the heart of a busy
and colourful shopping area dominated
by Indian-owned stores. There are

Juma Mosque, Durban

KwaZulu-Natal

Durban's popular 'Golden Mile' beachfront

several Hindu temples across the city and its outskirts, and the Alayam Hindu Temple provides an excellent example of temple architecture.
Contact KwaZulu-Natal Tourism for a comprehensive list. Tel: (031) 366 7500. www.kzn.org.za

NSA Gallery

The NSA Gallery is situated among large old trees in Bulwer Park, and is divided into three exhibition areas, which provide a platform for the work of many young local artists. Exhibitions change often, so it is best to check the latest programmes. There is also a gift shop and restaurant.
*Bulwer Road, Glenwood.
Tel: (031) 202 3686/7/8.
www.nsagallery.co.za.
Open: Mon–Fri 9am–5pm, Sat 9am–4pm, Sun 10am–3pm.*

The Golden Mile

This 6km (3³/₄-mile) stretch of beaches has for decades been the focal point of holidaymakers seeking safe swimming, good surfing and night-time entertainment. Fun fairs, shallow paddling pools and innumerable restaurants help entertain those tired of the sun and sea.

Fringed by many high-rise hotels, the area is very busy on holidays and weekends. Visitors should be cautious of pickpockets and under no circumstances walk along back streets.

At the northern end of the Golden Mile is the Fitzsimmons Snake Park, which has a good collection of South African reptiles. At the southern end of the 'Mile', uShaka Marine World has an excellent aquarium and dolphinarium (*see opposite*).

Fitzsimmons Snake Park

*Tel: 073 156 9606.
Open: Mon–Sun 9.30am–4.30pm.*

DIVING

The KwaZulu-Natal south coast has some excellent diving sites. On the Aliwal Shoal, divers are treated to regular sightings of ragged-tooth sharks, fearsome in appearance, but docile in nature, moray eels and innumerable reef fish.

Large numbers of fish are also attracted to several wrecked ships, which act as artificial reefs. Further north, Umkomaas also offers good diving, and there are several other deeper sites suitable for experienced divers.

Contact KwaZulu-Natal Tourism for a comprehensive list of operators and dive sites.
Tel: (031) 366 7500. www.kzn.org.za

*Demonstrations at regular intervals
throughout the day.
Admission charge.*

uShaka Marine World

The aquarium and dolphinarium
provide an exiting and comprehensive
insight into the sea-life of the warm
waters of South Africa's east coast.
Visitors can see sharks, turtles, dolphins
and a wide variety of deep- and
shallow-water fish, corals and seaweeds.

Displays include deep-water reefs
and an interactive tidal pool where
visitors are allowed to touch marine
creatures and seaweeds. There is also a
shipwreck reef. In this unique
environment, you have the opportunity
to snorkel with a huge variety of
marine life.

There are freshwater displays
focussing on the aquatic life
encountered in KwaZulu-Natal's rivers
and dams. Dolphin shows occur
regularly, and water slides and a variety
of other features provide entertainment
for children.

Diving on the Aliwal Shoal, KwaZulu-Natal

A spice shop in Victoria Street, Durban

*Located at the southern end of Golden
Mile. Tel: (031) 328 8000.
www.ushakamarineworld.co.za.
Open: winter Mon–Sun 9am–5pm,
summer Mon–Sun 9am–6pm.*

Victoria Street Market

This market is housed indoors but
surrounded by innumerable shops and
sidewalk stalls that stretch for several
city blocks.

A wide array of goods is available
within the market and everyone expects
to bargain. Spices, fabrics, Indian
jewellery, Zulu beadwork, elaborately
decorated spears, carved masks and
even fresh fish are available. In a
morning, visitors will meet an
intriguing cross-section of Durban's
residents.

Outside, street barbers offer quick
haircuts to customers waiting for
minibus taxis, while nearby vendors sell
woven mats, clothing and live chickens.
*Nearest corner: Queen St and Russell St.
Open: daily 6am–5pm.
Various tour operators.*

ANGLING

Both saltwater and freshwater angling enthusiasts will find ample opportunity to pursue their hobby in South Africa. Whether fishing from the beach for shad or grunter or from a boat for marlin and sailfish, anglers will be spoilt for choice. Saltwater fly-fishing is also widely followed, and the kingfish test even the best anglers.

Freshwater fly-fishing for trout has a large following, but recently the hard-fighting indigenous yellowfish is luring more and more anglers. Licences are required for all types of fishing but are easily acquired.

Wilson's Wharf and The Point

Both these areas are close to the city centre and offer good harbour views. A variety of restaurants and pubs create a pleasant setting for lunchtime or evening meals. Wilson's Wharf overlooks a yacht marina and also has a good range of craft and curio shops. The Point is a great vantage point from which to watch vessels, ranging from small fishing boats

The long coastline offers fine angling opportunities

to huge container ships, entering the port.

Wilson's Wharf
Boatman Street.

The Point
Off Point Road.
It is best to ask your hotel or tourist authorities for directions, and to arrange transport.

THE SOUTH COAST

The warm weather, laid-back attitude and good beaches make the South Coast a favourite holiday and retirement destination for many South Africans.

This region runs for 160km (100 miles) south of Durban and, in addition to its beaches and seafood restaurants, has several crocodile farms, markets and good golf courses.

The Oribi Gorge Nature Reserve has about 35km (20 miles) of trails that wind in and out of a forested gorge, and fortunate visitors might spot some of the antelope and monkeys that live here.

The narrow-gauge Banana Express steam train runs from Port Shepstone to the Orbi Gorge Nature Reserve. The trip makes a good day outing, particularly for children (*see p46*).
For **Banana Express** *bookings call* **Port Shepstone Publicity.**
Tel: (039) 682 4821. Call to confirm schedule.

Riverbend Croc Farm
Tel: (039) 316 6204.
Open: Mon–Sun 9am–5pm.

THE NORTH COAST

The North Coast has been heavily developed in recent years with a string of upmarket hotels and holiday developments running for some 50km (30 miles) north of Durban.

It is a good place for an easily arranged stress-free holiday with plenty of safe swimming beaches, good restaurants and other entertainment. Dolphins are often spotted along this coast, hence its popular name of the Dolphin Coast.

Dolphin Coast Publicity Association
Tel: (032) 946 1997.
www.dolphincoast.kzn.org.za

Zulu man in traditional dress

Natal Sharks Board

Sharks are widely feared, but most people's terror is based on misconceptions. The Board offers comprehensive audio-visual displays and lectures, dispelling some of the myths about these creatures which fill an important ecological niche. Sharks caught in the shark nets that protect many beaches are sometimes dissected during tours.

The board is situated at Umhlanga Rocks some 20km (12 miles) north of Durban. They monitor the shark nets that protect many of KwaZulu-Natal's bathing beaches, and boat tours can be arranged.

Natal Sharks Board
Tel: (031) 566 0400.
Open: Mon–Thur & Sun with three shows daily. Times vary so call for details.
Admission charge.

Shakaland

Shakaland offers an 'interactive' experience of life in a Zulu kraal a hundred years ago. Zulu warriors with shields and spears dance for guests, storytellers recount tales of kings and queens, and guides explain local traditions. Overnight accommodation is provided in traditional 'beehive huts' made of grass woven over wooden poles. Authentic traditional food including the staple *phutu* (a stiff porridge made from de-husked maize), and indigenous vegetables are also available but not compulsory.

Shakaland is some 162km (100 miles) north of Durban near the town of Eshowe.
Tel: (035) 460 0912 to arrange visits and book accommodation.
Opens at 11am.
Admission charge.

Game Reserves of Zululand and Maputaland

The spectacular game reserves of Zululand offer protection to a bewildering array of animals, birds, fish and plant life, and help make the region one of South Africa's top wildlife areas.

These reserves are some of the oldest in Africa. Hluhluwe Imfolozi Park was created as two separate parks in 1896, and has been the core of more than 100 years of pioneering conservation work, including the epic effort that saved the white rhino from extinction.

In the Greater St Lucia Wetlands Park, elephants and black rhinos browse within sight of hippos and crocodiles. A few kilometres away, the warm Indian Ocean nurtures coral reefs and prolific sea life including humpback whale passing by on the annual migration.

The lake, which is really an estuary and one of the largest in Africa, is surrounded by varying forms of forest, grasslands and woodlands. In addition to the elephants and rhinos, these areas support buffalo, leopard, zebra, reedbuck and many other species of mammal, as well as prolific birdlife.

High, forested sand dunes, among the highest in the world, roll down

See leather-back turtles on the beaches at Greater St Lucia Wetlands Park

The Greater St Lucia Wetand Park has a large crocodile population

right to the edge of wide, sandy beaches. In summer, the beaches are used as nesting sites by logger-head turtles and huge leather-back turtles (really big specimens can weigh 600kg/1,320lb). The turtles lay their eggs towards the end of the year. Just over two months later, the babies make their first foray into the sea. Authorities run strictly controlled tours to watch both the nesting and hatching processes.

Various coral reefs fringe the shoreline, providing excellent snorkelling and diving.

There are several other parks along the coast including Kosi Bay and Mapelane. Kosi Bay is one of the most important estuary systems in the country, and is an important nursery for marine fish. There are also coral reefs at the mouth of the system, which consists of four lakes of increasing salinity.

Further inland, neighbouring Mkhuze Game Reserve and the Phongola Biosphere Reserve offer protection to a wide range of species and habitat.

Not far away is Hluhluwe Imfolozi Park where conservationists managed to save the white rhino from possible extinction. These large, docile creatures had been hunted mercilessly until the 1920s, by which time their numbers had dwindled to a few dozen.

A few far-sighted conservationists pressed for a special programme to protect the white rhino, and also the black, and today South Africa is the stronghold of the world population. Worldwide some 11,000 white rhinos live in the wild and in zoos, but only about 3,300 black rhinos exist.

The area between the Black Umfolozi and White Umfolozi rivers was once the hunting ground of the Zulu King Shaka, and was off limits to commoners and outsiders. This restriction helped maintain the wildlife population before the first White settlers arrived.

Other protected areas include the mountainous Ithala Game Reserve and the Ndumo Game Reserve, which are two of the country's top birding spots with more than 400 species having been recorded. There are many privately run game reserves and lodges throughout the region, which also offer excellent accommodation and good game viewing.
Tel: (033) 845 1000.
www.kznwildlife.com

RESERVES AND PARKS
Hluhluwe Imfolozi Park

There is no easier place in the world to see rhinos in the wild. Around 1,200 white and 300 black rhino live in the park which constitutes one-tenth of the global population, and that's including those animals in captivity.

All the other members of the Big Five occur, as well as large populations of giraffe, nyala and other species. The Mpila and Hilltop camps offer accommodation ranging from self-catering in safari tents to upmarket, fully serviced lodges. There are also several 'bush lodges' which are set away from the main camps.

Short walks with skilled guides can be arranged and should not be missed. Longer three- and four-day trails, where walkers camp in the bush, are also on offer. Night drives can be booked and are another 'must do', as they enable visitors to see many nocturnal species that might otherwise be missed.

Greater St Lucia Wetland Park

This World Heritage site is actually an amalgamation of several reserves. It encompasses a wide range of habitats, including the huge Lake St Lucia beaches, coral reefs, grasslands and woodlands. Elephants, rhino, buffalo and antelope occur on the shores of the lake, and the reefs offer excellent diving and snorkelling. Bird life is exceptional. The beaches are broad and clean, and the water is warm nearly all year round.

Accommodation ranges from comfortable lodges to camping, and many companies arrange tours. Sodwana Bay provides the easiest access points to the best coral reefs. There are self-catering chalets and privately run lodges and other accommodation nearby.

Ithala Game Reserve

Although less well known than some of the other parks, Ithala nevertheless is well worth visiting for its variety of habitat alone. The landscape is extremely rugged, and high mountains drop steeply down to the hot valley of the Phongola River.

Elephant, rhino and buffalo are regularly spotted, and the reserve is an excellent place to see the nocturnal aardwolf which, although it is as big as a medium-sized dog, lives on ants. The award-winning Ntshondwe Camp is built on the side of the Ngotshe mountains.

Ndumo and Mkhuze Game Reserves

Both the reserves offer excellent game viewing and are two of South Africa's premier birding sites. Ndumo is located on the border of Mozambique, and its many pans (small natural lakes), fringed with the yellow-barked fever trees, create a sense of tropical Africa. Thick forest and dense reed beds add to the atmosphere of adventure.

Although neither reserve is very large, they are both enormously diverse. *Parks open all year round.*

Contact **Ezemvelo KZN Wildlife**
Tel: (033) 845 1000.
www. kznwildlife.com
Contact **KZN Tourism** *for a*
comprehensive list of private reserves
and lodges.
Tel: (031) 366 7500.
www.kzn.org.za

The uKhahlamba-Drakensberg Park

This 250,000-hectare (620,000-acre) Park is also a World Heritage Site, and throughout the mountain range sheer cliffs, steep sandstone-fringed foothills and cold, clear streams create a peaceful world far removed from the hustle and bustle of cities.

Summers are warm with regular thunderstorms. Winters can be icy with occasional snowfalls, and many high-altitude streams freeze at night. Peaks here average over 3,000m (9,840ft).

The entire range offers excellent hiking, walks, horse riding and birding. Large game is scarce at high altitude but many small species do occur. The rare bearded vulture is often seen as are black eagles, lanner falcons and a host of smaller birds.

These mountains proved to be one of the last refuges of the San (Bushmen).

Champagne Castle, uKhahlamba-Drakensberg mountains

Hundreds of their rock paintings and engravings can be found in the caves and rock shelters of the foothills known as the 'Little Berg'.

There are plenty of hotels, B&Bs and guest farms dotted along the entire length of the mountain range, and these offer a wide range of activities including tennis, fly-fishing, mountain-bike riding, abseiling and other sports. The Park is comprised of many smaller reserves including those listed below.

Didima (Cathedral Peak)

Didima offers the best of both worlds – the outdoor splendour of the mountains and the luxurious comfort of imaginatively designed chalets and restaurant.

There is a comprehensive San art interpretive centre where the long, and sometimes sad, history of the San is explained. The display also explains the

No need to worry – the Cannibal Cave hiking trail is great fun

spiritual role art played in the life of these nomadic hunters.

For the fit, there are day hikes to the top of Cathedral Peak. Many easier walks are, however, accessible, and if the going gets too hot, a plunge into a mountain pool is likely to invigorate even the most weary of hikers.

Giant's Castle

Set above the clear Bushman's River, the main rest camp has spectacular views of the high, blue-grey walls and peaks of the uKhahlamba-Drakensberg (*uKhahlamba* means 'barrier of spears' in Zulu and *Drakensberg* means 'dragon mountain' in Afrikaans).

The San once hunted eland and other animals in the deep valleys beneath 'the Giant'. Hundreds of their rock paintings and engravings can be found in many caves and rock shelters in the area. One of the best collections is at the main caves just a short walk from the comfortable main camp.

Visitors spend time hiking, horse riding, trout fishing or simply relaxing at the edge of a mountain stream or in the quiet gardens of the rest camp itself. Injisuthi camp, further north, offers self-catering chalets and tents in a remote valley surrounded by sandstone cliffs.

Royal Natal and Rugged Glen

The breathtaking 5km- (3 mile-) long sheer wall of the Amphitheatre is the focal point of Royal Natal. The Thukela River starts life high on the summit

The rolling sugar-cane fields and plantations of the KwaZulu-Natal Midlands

before tumbling down sheer cliffs to form one of the highest waterfalls in the world.

Royal Natal offers the tranquillity found throughout the 'Berg' and is one of South Africa's most popular mountain destinations. Hikes and walks ranging from a few hours to several days can be undertaken along well-marked paths, and trout fishing and horse riding are also very popular.

Elsewhere in the Berg

There are other provincial parks including the Coleford, Kamberg and Loteni nature reserves, as well as dozens of private hotels, guest farms and B&Bs.

The Giant's Cup and Mkhomazi Wilderness Areas offer exhilarating hiking along the face of the mountains, with overnight stops in caves or mountain huts. These hikes are for the fit only, but well worth the time and effort.

Parks open all year round.
Contact **Ezemvelo KZN Wildlife**
Tel: (033) 845 1011.
www. kznwildlife.com
Contact **KZN Tourism** *for a list of private lodges, B&Bs, campsites and tours.*
Tel: (031) 366 7500.
www.kzn.org.za

THE MIDLANDS

Set among the lush green hills, the Midlands Meander arts and craft route runs through some of KwaZulu-Natal's most beautiful scenery. More than 160 craft shops, art galleries, restaurants, hotels, and B&Bs are scattered along country roads beginning about 25km (15 miles) north of Pietermaritzburg.

The Valley of a Thousand Hills near Durban

Boer Voorterkkers fleeing British rule in 1838. The British took over the city in 1843, and it became the capital of the Colony of Natal. The city still has many buildings dating from the 19th century, including the all-brick City Hall, the Old Natal Parliament and the railway station. Seventy of these buildings are national monuments, and self-guided trails enable visitors to see many of them in a few hours walk.

The Voortrekker Museum housed in the small gabled Church of the Vow was erected in 1841 by the Boers. It commemorates the Battle of Blood River, and depicts life during that time.

The area is ideal for weekends spent wandering along, while shopping and stopping for tea, lunch or dinner. Just outside the town of Howick, the Umgeni River tumbles over the 95m-(312ft-) high Howick Falls. At nearby Midmar Dam and the surrounding nature reserve there is an historical village and open-air museum. The area offers good water sports, riding and game viewing.

It is best to visit the Meander website or to get a copy of their extensive brochure to plan your trip according to your tastes.

Midlands Meander Association
Tel: (033) 330 8195.
www.midlandsmeander.co.za

PIETERMARITZBURG

This sleepy city is the capital of the province, and was established by the

Carpets for sale in the Midlands

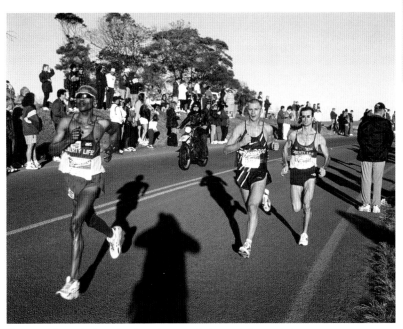

The annual Comrades Marathon is run between Durban and Pietermaritzburg

The nearby Natal Museum is devoted to the region's social and natural history. The Tatham Art Gallery contains European and South African works, and there are also a number of interesting churches, mosques and Hindu temples in the city.

Pietermaritzburg Tourism
177 Commercial Rd. Tel: (033) 345 1348.
www.pmbtourism.co.za

Tatham Art Gallery
Tel: (033) 392 2801.
Open: Tue–Sun 10am–6pm.

Voortrekker Museum
351 Longmarket St. Tel: (033) 394 6834.
Open: Mon–Fri 9am–4pm, Sat
9am–1pm.

Natal Museum
237 Loop St.
Tel: (033) 345 1404. Open: Mon–Fri
9am–4.30pm, Sat 10am–4pm, Sun
11am–3pm.

GANDHI

Pietermaritzburg played an ungracious but important role in the early life of Indian pacifist, Mohandas Gandhi (later known as Mahatma). In 1893, he was evicted from the first-class carriage of a train at Pietermaritzburg Station because of his race. He later said the incident triggered his philosophy of passive resistance based on truth and compassion.

Gandhi became an international symbol of passive resistance, and a statue in his memory was erected outside the Old Colonial Building in 1993.

Tour: KwaZulu-Natal battlefields

Some of the fiercest battles ever fought in South Africa raged across the hills and valleys of KwaZulu-Natal throughout the 19th century, leaving thousands of dead Zulu, British and Boer soldiers, women and children.

Allow two days. Start at Spioenkop, which is about 150km (94 miles) north of Pietermartizburg on the N3 freeway. At the N11 junction turn left to Spioenkop which is about 18km (12 miles) west of the freeway.

Early Boer settlers clashed several times with Zulu armies in the late 1830s. In 1879, the ferocious Anglo-Zulu War erupted. During the South African War (Anglo-Boer War) of 1899–1902, some of the worst fighting took place in KwaZulu-Natal. Dozens of other battles also took place.

1 Spioenkop
Earlier British forces sent to relieve Ladysmith fought a bitter battle against the Boers for the strategic mountain of Spioenkop which overlooks Ladysmith.
Spioenkop walk and tape tours available. Tel: (036) 488 1578.
Open: daily 6am–6pm.
Ladysmith Siege Museum
Tel: (036) 637 2992.
Open: Mon–Fri 9am–4pm, Sat 9am–1pm.
Retrace your route to the N3, and Ladysmith is a further 14km (9 miles) to the east along the N11.

2 Siege of Ladysmith
In one of the most famous battles of the South African War, Boer commandos surrounded British forces in Ladysmith and kept them trapped there for 118 days. The water supply ran out, food shortages became acute and disease broke out, killing many in the town. Both defenders and attackers took heavy casualties in the fighting until the town was relieved on 28 February 1900.
From Ladysmith take the N11 north for about 75km (47 miles) until the junction with the R68 to Dundee. Follow the R68 for 22km (13 miles). The battlefield is on the eastern side of the town.

3 Talana battlefield
This was the scene of the first battle between the British and Boers in 1899. The Boers won the battle, and the British retreated to Ladysmith where they were later trapped. Graves and monuments mark the site of the

British graves at the Talana Hill battlesite, KwaZulu-Natal

Isandhlwana, the site of a famous Zulu victory over the British

battle. There is also a museum that documents Dundee's history as a coal mining and glass-manufacturing town.

Talana Museum

Tel: (034) 212 2654.

www.talana.co.za.

Choice of guided and self-guided tours of battlefield.

Tourism Dundee

Tel: (034) 212 2121. Open: Mon–Fri 8am–4.30pm. Sat, Sun & public holidays 10am–4pm. Closed: Christmas Day.

It is about 45km (28 miles) from Dundee to Rorke's Drift on the R68. Follow the signs to Isandhlwana which is about 30km (18 miles) further.

4 Isandhlwana and Rorke's Drift

On 22 January 1879 the Zulu Army, although later vanquished, inflicted the largest ever defeat on the British colonial army at Isandhlwana. More than 870 British soldiers were killed.

Several Zulu regiments then moved on to attack Rorke's Drift where a small number of men fought vastly superior forces for more than 12 hours. Eleven of the defenders later received the Victoria Cross, Britain's highest award for bravery.

There is a good arts and crafts centre over the road from the museum.

Isandhlwana Battle site enquiries.

Tel: (034) 271 0634.

Open: all week, but call first.

Rorke's Drift Museum

Tel: (034) 642 1687.

Open: all week, but call first.

From Rorke's Drift, follow the road back to the R68, and then head towards

Dundee. The Blood River turnoff is 27km (16 miles) east of Dundee on the R33, and the battlefield a further 20km (12 miles) southeast.

5 Blood River/Ncome

This battle forms one of the cornerstones of Afrikaner history. Today the 1838 battlefield is a hallowed spot for some Afrikaners, who believe that their God supported them in defeating the Zulus.

The battle was the result of an attempt to punish the Zulus for what the Voortrekkers believed to be the murder of one of their leaders. A small Voortrekker party took on a far superior Zulu force and won. There is a replica *laager* (circle) of 68 wagons commemorating the Boer victory, and also a monument to the Zulu soldiers who died.

Ncome Museum
Tel: (034) 271 8121.
www.ncomemusuem.co.za.
Open: Mon–Sun 8am–4pm.

The Museum at Rorke's Drift, KwaZulu-Natal

Tour: Old Zulu Kingdom

Old Zululand covered a vast tract of central KwaZulu-Natal. One of the most interesting sections lies north of Durban, particularly between the Tugela River and the Swazi border. Here there are Zulu homesteads, historic battlegrounds, memorials and forts.

Allow at least 2 days. Start at Stanger and drive up the N2 for 56km (35 miles) to Gingindlovu.

1 Gingindlovu

Gingindlovu (swallower of the elephant) was the site of a military *kraal* (settlement) built by Cetshwayo (Shaka's nephew) to commemorate victory over his brother, Mbulazi, in their contest for the Zulu throne. The *kraal* was destroyed by the British in 1879.
From Gingindlovu, take the R66 to Eshowe (26km/16 miles).

2 Eshowe

Eshowe (sound of wind in the trees) was a quiet summer retreat for the Zulus. Shaka's Kraal overlooks Nkwalini Valley. Cetshwayo's first *kraal* was here in 1860, before he moved to Ulundi. It was

Zulu crafts

replaced by the British-built Fort Nongqai (1883), now the Zululand Historical Museum. Near Nkandla Forest Reserve (place of exhaustion) is the grave of Cetshwayo who died in 1884.
For Shaka's Kraal, take the R68 north from Eshowe (6km/4 miles), right on the R230 (dirt road) for about 20km (12 miles).

Continue along the R68 to Melmoth (27km/17 miles), then turn onto the R34 and continue for 24km (15 miles) to uMgungundlovu.

3 uMgungundlovu

Dingane moved the Zulu capital from KwaDukuza to uMgungundlovu (place of the great elephant), where Voortrekker leader Piet Retief and his men were executed in February 1838. Retribution was grim: 3,000 warriors were killed at the Battle of Blood River (*see p81*).

The uMgungundlovu Museum occupies the site of the *kraal*, the core of which has been accurately rebuilt. *Take the R66 to Ulundi (about 18km/ 11 miles).*

4 Ulundi

It was customary for a newly crowned king to establish his own capital: Ulundi was Cetshwayo's (1873). The British destroyed it in 1879, finally breaking Zulu military power. A second capital at Ondini (the heights) was burned by the Swazis. The local government rebuilt it as the KwaZulu Cultural Museum, and the royal quarters have been re-created. Close to

Ulundi, is the eMakhosini Valley and royal burial ground. From Ulundi, the route branches east, passing through the Hluhluwe Imfolozi Park (*see p72*). *Leave the park on the R618 access road and, at the junction with the N2, head south and back via Stanger to Durban.*

Fort Nonqai

Nonqai Road. Tel: (035) 474 4976. Open: Mon–Sat 9am–4pm.

KwaZulu Cultural Museum

3km (2 miles) east of town at Ondini. Tel: (035) 870 2050. www.heritage.co.za. Open: Mon–Fri 9.30am–5pm. Admission charge for both museums.

Limpopo

Most people in this province derive their livelihoods from agriculture and the wildlife industry. The northern half of the Kruger National Park is in Limpopo, but there are many smaller reserves and private game ranches scattered throughout the province. Many of the ranches cater for the hunting industry which attracts many foreign clients. Every Easter, more than a million pilgrims visit the Zionist Christian Church headquarters at Moria, near the capital city Polokwane.

Tzaneen and Magoebaskloof

The cold trout streams of the Magoebaskloof Pass drop steeply down to the sub-tropical mango, avocado pear and litchi farms around Tzaneen. Tzaneen is in a transition zone between the hot Lowveld and cooler Highveld.

The game ranches that border the Kruger National Park begin east of Tzaneen, and to the northeast is the Modjadji Forest, home to the huge Modjadji palm, a form of cycad which

Ndebele pots

The fertile Magoebaskloof valley

evolved over 50 million years ago and grows to a height of some 13m (42ft). The area is also home to the Modjaji Rain Queen, a descendant of a 16th century Karanga princess, who is reputed to know the secrets of making

NDEBELE ART

Their extraordinary art is the single aspect of South Ndebele culture that distinguishes it from that of other Nguni groups. Usually referred to simply as Ndebele, the South Ndebele live for the most part in the Limpopo Highveld, northeast of Pretoria.

From house painting to beadwork, mural painting to the elaborate traditional dress style of the women, the Ndebele's striking attention to colour and pattern and their sense of symmetry are unusual. The palette of the original Ndebele house painters was restricted to ochre, natural clays and charcoals. Their beadwork has considerable cultural significance. Specific designs and garments are reserved for, as an example, married women, and others for widows.

rain. People still consult the Queen and ply her with gifts to bring good rains.

Soutpansberg

In the far north of the Limpopo Province, the Soutpansberg mountains form an enormously biologically diverse zone. The southern slopes of the mountains are among some of the wettest in South Africa. The northern slopes are however dry, and soon give way to the plains and the giant baobab trees that are so characteristic of the Limpopo River Valley.

There are many private game lodges and reserves in the mountains and on the surrounding plains. Hiking trails and game viewing dominate activities in this area, which is also an important tropical fruit-farming region.

The region is also the home of the Venda people who settled here in the 18th century. Many sites in the area are sacred. At Dsatza are ruins of ancient stone structures, and Lake Fundudzi is believed to be the home of a python god.

The baobab tree, a resident of the hot north

Mpumalanga

The Kruger National Park is Mpumalanga's most famous attraction, but the province also has some of the best trout fishing in South Africa, many smaller game parks and wonderful scenery. Just over 120 years ago, the hills around Barberton and Pilgrim's Rest were the focus of a frenzied gold rush. Museums in many towns exhibit memories of the South African War (1899–1902). Shangaan culture is also highlighted in several art galleries and cultural villages.

Barberton

Barberton was founded after the discovery of gold. Its fame, however, was short lived, as the far richer finds on the Witwatersrand caused an almost immediate exodus of fortune seekers. Many of the town's old buildings survived, including the Kaap Gold Fields' Stock Exchange, the Transvaal's first stock exchange, and the 1887 Globe Tavern, a hostelry of a type common in the goldfields of the late 19th century.

The Barberton Museum contains artefacts relating to the gold rush days.

Barberton in Mpumalanga

In Barberton Park there is a statue of the dog Jock, the subject of Sir Percy FitzPatrick's famous story, *Jock of the Bushveld*. Many people hike or ride horses in the hills around Barberton.

Barberton Information Bureau
Tel: (013) 712 2121.

Dullstroom

Dullstroom has become a trendy weekend getaway destination, and is the centre of the thriving trout-fishing industry. Many people visit the area to simply walk in the hills and to spend a quiet weekend at one of the wide range of guest farms or lodges. Others pursue the brown and rainbow trout with passion. A wide range of craft shops and restaurants has been established in the village and surrounding areas.

Nearby Lydenberg is also an important fly-fishing area.

Dullstroom Accommodation
Tel: (013) 254 0020.
www.dullstroom.co.za

Hazyview

Shangana Cultural Village

Dressed in traditional skins and headdresses, Shangana dancers and storytellers recount some of the legends of their people and region at this village close to the borders of the Kruger National Park. Curios made by local people are also sold at The Marula Market in the village.

Hazyview.
Tel: (013) 737 7000.
www.shangana.co.za.
Open: daily, but contact them for performance times.

Nelspruit and White River

Nelspruit is the largest town and capital of Mpumalanga. It is also the gateway to the Lowveld.

The Lowveld National Botanical Gardens are well worth visiting, and have an impressive collection of cycads and other Lowveld flowers and trees.

Nearby is the sub-tropical town of White River where mangos, avocados and other fruit are grown. Soon after White River, the orchards begin to make way for game-ranching land.

Lowveld National Botanical Gardens
Tel: (013) 752 5531.
www.nbi.ac.za

Sudwala Caves

West of Nelspruit on the slopes of the Northern Drakensberg are the Sudwala Caves. Visitors are only allowed to pass through the first few hundred metres, and the total depth of the cavern system is still uncertain.

Within the cave are bizarre rock formations, spectacular stalactites and stalagmites and fossils of prehistoric algae. Below the entrance to the caves there is a restaurant and an open-air museum with some life-size replicas of dinosaurs and other prehistoric creatures.

Mpumalanga Tourism Authority
Tel: (013) 752 7001.
www.mpumalanga.com

Pilgrim's Rest

Kruger National Park

Pretoriuskop Camp in the Kruger

Sprawling across a vast expanse of hot, game-rich bush and woodland, cut by four major rivers and bordered by two others, is the Kruger National Park. The park is one of Africa's premier wildlife areas and tourist destinations. The park covers some 20,000sq km (7,722sq miles), and there are 25 camps offering many types of accommodation.

There are several top-of-the-range, privately run lodges too. Each rest camp offers something different in the way of scenery, and the game and birdlife varies according to habitat.

The view from the Olifants thatched camp, high on the hill overlooking the Olifants River, is spectacular. Visitors get eye-level views of circling marabou storks and vultures, while far below elephants browse among the knob thorn and mopane trees.

Further south near Skukuza, the largest camp in the park, wild dogs are often spotted, and lucky visitors sometimes see these rare predators hunting, their white-tipped tails streaming behind them as they chase their quarry through the bush. Almost 500 species of bird occur in the park. Many species of mammals, reptiles, trees and even insects keep hefty guidebooks busy.

The area covered by Kruger also has a rich human history. Near Pafuri, the stone citadel of Thulamela, which has now been restored to its former glory, dates back to the Late Iron Age. It was an important cultural and trading settlement with links to other stone cities like Great Zimbabwe. A vital component in southern African and worldwide conservation, Kruger attracts more than a million visitors a year.

Recently, fences between the Kruger National Park and a conservation area in neighbouring Mozambique have been taken down, enabling the formation of the Great Limpopo Transfrontier Park. Similarly, fences have been taken down along the western boundary of the Kruger National Park. This allows the free movement of game from well-run, upmarket private game reserves developed along the park's boundary.

Kruger tips:

- If you are on a self-drive trip in the Kruger National Park, plan your day carefully. Distances are considerable, and game viewing takes time.

- All camp gates are locked at last light and only opened again at daybreak.

- The speed limit on tar roads is 50kph (30mph), and on gravel roads it is 40kph (25mph). Authorities set up speed traps and issue fines in an attempt to control speeding. Cars kill hundreds of wild animals and birds annually.

- In summer, it is best to get up at first-light and travel in the cool of the morning. Return to camp for a brunch and siesta in the middle of the day, when the temperatures can climb dramatically. Go out on another game drive after 3pm.

- Make sure to book a night drive with a trained guide – private individuals are not allowed to drive outside the camps at night.

- Talk to other guests and park staff about game sightings. It will help you plan your viewing, although there is no guarantee that the animals will be in the same place.

- Take adequate supplies of food and drink with you when you set off on a drive.

A lion cub

The 'Big Five'

The 'Big Five' are the trump cards of African game reserves. Everyone wants to see them. The 'Big Five' are the lion, elephant, rhinoceros, leopard and buffalo. The term has an unfortunate origin – to early hunters these were considered to be the most dangerous animals to kill, and in some instances the hunters did become the hunted with fatal consequences.

Today these animals are considered hugely important in the tourism industry, and have status that would have shocked people 100 years ago. In many instances they were considered to be, at best, pests and, in some instances, vermin.

The Big Five
Lion
Research shows that tourists like to watch these animals more than any other species. They are the only communal large cats and live in prides that sometimes exceed 20 animals.

Large males weigh over 200kg (440lb) and females average around 130kg (286lb). They often hunt co-operatively, some animals flushing prey and others making the kill.

Popular myth has it that males simply eat whatever lionesses kill, but the reality is that they are fearsome predators and often kill for themselves. They usually hunt under cover of darkness.

Elephant
Elephants are the second most-popular animals amongst visitors to Africa. Male elephants are huge, and some mature bulls weigh over

6,500kg (14,300lb) and stand about 3.3m (10ft 9in) at the shoulder. Females are considerably smaller.

They are entirely vegetarian and eat leaves, fruit, bark, grass and other vegetable matter. They have a considerable impact on their environment due to their habit of pushing over trees to get at succulent new leaves and twigs. Female matriarchs lead all herds, but mature bulls visit regularly to mate.

Rhinoceros

Two species, the black and the white, occur in southern Africa. The white rhino is the larger of the two, bulls weigh up to 2,600kg (5,730lb), whereas the black rhino seldom weighs more than 1,200kg (2,640lb). The black rhino has a reputation for being bad tempered and charging without warning, but they usually only do so when they feel threatened.

The black rhino is endangered, with only about 3,300 individuals left in the wild and captivity worldwide.

Leopard

Leopards are usually secretive animals and sometimes live close to human settlements for years without being detected. These solitary carnivores are remarkably strong for their size. Males weigh about 80–90kg (176–198lb), and hunt by sight and hearing. They are quite capable of killing animals much larger than themselves.

Leopards are exceptionally patient hunters and will spend long periods crouching motionless while watching their prey. These spotted cats are extremely beautiful, and once seen in the wild are seldom forgotten.

African buffalo

Although they may look like large, docile cows, buffalo can be extremely aggressive and often drive off lions attacking a herd member. Lone bulls are notoriously short-tempered, and walking through thick bush when they are around can be a nerve-racking experience.

They weigh between 700–800kg (1,540–1,760lb).

Tour: Northern Drakensberg Mountains

This tour winds through the Northern Drakensberg mountains, and takes in a series of spectacular vistas of the mountains and the Lowveld far below. Along the way, there are many opportunities to stop for a snack or shop.

The tour is suitable for a self-drive trip, although several companies offer tours that follow a similar route.

Allow a full day. Start at Sabie, and head north past Graskop along the edge of the escarpment on the R37, and then along the R532 to the Blyde River Canyon.

1 Sabie and Graskop

The pleasant village of Sabie is the centre of a thriving commercial forestry industry. There are several high waterfalls in the area including the Bridal Veil Falls (70m/230ft), the Lone Creek Falls (68m/223ft) and the Mac Mac Falls (64m/210ft) near Graskop.

The Forestry Museum in Sabie tells the story of the industry in the area.

An old miner's house, which is now a shop, in Pilgrim's Rest

Graskop, 29km (18 miles) to the north was once a gold-mining settlement, but is today also closely linked to the forestry industry and tourism. Be sure to stop and enjoy the magnificent view of the Blyde River Canyon from the God's Window view site near Graskop. *Beyond God's Window, the R532 continues past the Bourke's Luck Potholes, which have been ground into the rock by the swirling waters. There are viewing platforms here. The road continues to the Blydepoort Nature Reserve.*

2 Blyde River Canyon and Blydepoort Nature Reserve

The Blyde River gouges its way through the mountains, and has created a 20km- (12-mile-) long canyon that is 800m (2,600ft) deep in places. There are any number of panoramic views here, and dominating the area are three

Lisbon Falls near Graskop

peaks known as the Three Sisters (also known as the Three Rondavels). The Lisbon and Berlin falls are nearby.

The area around the dam that has been created in the canyon is a nature reserve, and there is a wide variety of hiking trails that wind along the face of the mountains. There is accommodation to suit all tastes throughout the area.

From Blydepoort the road heads north to the junction of the R36. Turn left here onto the R36 towards Ohrigstad.

Close to the junction is the road to the Echo Caves.

3 Echo Caves

The sequence of chambers in the Molopong Valley has yielded a rich collection of Middle and Late Stone Age implements. There is an open-air display of archaeological implements.

Follow the R36 to Ohrigstad and then take the R533 to Pilgrim's Rest.

4 Pilgrim's Rest

This entire village has been declared a national monument. It was the scene of a gold rush after Alec 'Wheelbarrow' Patterson found alluvial deposits of the

Roadside hawker selling his zebras

Dustbin at the God's Window view site

precious metal here in 1887. Much of the town has been preserved in its original state, and the main road is lined with red and white corrugated-iron buildings.

The post-office building and other museums house memorabilia of the gold-rush era. Many of the stores in the town sell curios and artwork.

Pilgrim's Rest Tourist Information
Tel: (013) 768 1471.

Continue on the R533 until it joins the R534 back to Graskop.

ROADSIDE HAWKERS

In many parts of South Africa hawkers sell curios and other goods at the roadside. Many offer prices much lower than established shops. It is, however, wise to check wooden carvings, especially the larger items, for cracks or splits. In some cases, shoe polish is used to hide the cracks.

Many of the carvings, particularly those of giraffes, are designed to stand, but check the bases to make sure they are flat. In some cases they may seem perfectly OK at the roadside but are, in reality, craftily supported with stones or sticks.

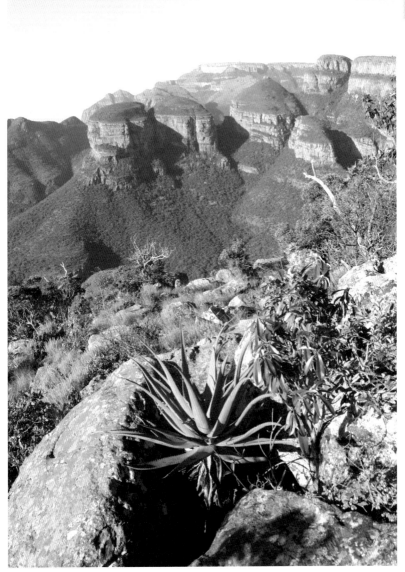

The Three Rondavels (huts) in the Blydepoort Nature Reserve

North West

The Pilanesberg and Madikwe Game Reserves and the Sun City golf course and entertainment complex are the tourism hubs of this rural province. All three destinations are close enough to Johannesburg and Pretoria for quick visits. Both game reserves are relatively small and have thriving populations of the Big Five and other animals, which usually ensures good game viewing. Platinum mining, farming and tourism are the major economic activities of the province.

Pilanesberg National Park

Situated around the remains of an ancient volcano, this park provides the closest Big Five game viewing to Johannesburg, which is just two hours away by road.

The reserve was formed with the purchase of cattle farms in the 1970s and restocked with wild game, one of the largest operations of its kind ever undertaken. A network of good roads and large animal populations usually ensure good game viewing. A wide range of accommodation is available.

Game Viewing Hide, Mankwe Dam, Pilanesberg National Park

Weekends have become very busy, because the reserve is so close to Johannesburg and Pretoria.

Pilanesberg National Park
170km (105 miles) west of Johannesburg.
Tel: (014) 555 5354.
Open: all year round.

Sun City

This complex of hotels, casinos and golf courses is South Africa's answer to Las Vegas. The expensive Lost City complex is a fantasyland of carved animals and an opulent, palace-like hotel. The older Sun City has similar, if less grand, facilities and the Valley of the Waves water attraction provides a seaside experience, complete with artificially generated breakers, for children hundreds of kilometres from the nearest ocean.

Both complexes have world-class golf courses, and in December some of the world best players compete here for a vast amount of prize money.

Lost City complex

The complex is on the borders of the Pilanesberg National Park.

Sun City Resort
Tel: (011) 557 1000.
www.suninternational.com

The Waterberg

For decades, most tourists, including South Africans, ignored this rugged region. However, with the development of a new national park and a whole range of private game reserves, it is starting to get the attention it deserves.

Although the Marakele National Park is still in the early stages of development, it shares a boundary with the Welgevonden complex of private game reserves. Together the two form a malaria-free Big Five wildlife area with good game viewing.

Further north, the Lapalala Wilderness has established itself as an excellently run private reserve, and the Touchstone Ranch offers horseback safari amongst wild game.

Waterberg Tourism Association
Tel: (014) 755 3535.
www.waterbergtourism.com

Madikwe Game Reserve

This is another game reserve that was formerly cattle farms, that has been restocked with game including the Big Five. It is also malaria free. Although self-drive visits are not allowed, there are several lodges in the reserve, and all offer day and night drives with trained guides.

The area is hot in summer and has mild winter days.

Madikwe Game Reserve
Tel: (018) 3672 and ask for 2411, or view the following websites:

The Bush House
www.madikwehouse.co.za

Etali Safari Lodge
www.etalisafari.co.za

Jaci's Safari Lodge
www.madikwe.com

Madikwe River Lodge
www.country-escapes.co.za/madik.htm

Mateya Safari Lodge
www.mateyasafari.co.za

Mosetlha Bush Camp
www.thebushcamp.com

Tau Game Lodge
www.taugamelodge.co.za

18th hole at Sun City golf course

Northern Cape

The Northern Cape is South Africa's most sparsely populated province, and shares remote borders with Namibia and Botswana. The province is primarily a sheep and cattle farming region, although Kimberley, the largest city, owes its existence to the rich deposits of diamonds first found there over 130 years ago. Near Kimberley are the important South African War battle sites of Modder River and Magersfontein. The huge Kgalagadi Transfrontier Park to the north is a premier tourist destination.

Kimberley

In July 1871, the first diamonds were discovered at Colesberg Kopje (a *kopje* is a small hill), around which Kimberley, initially a tent-town of fortune seekers, sprung up.

The entire hill was dug away as miners found more and more diamonds. In later years even more miners continued digging straight down until they had created Kimberley's famous 'Big Hole', which is 800m (2,624ft) deep. More than 14 million carats of diamonds were extracted.

Today, it is part of an open museum, which incorporates entire streets of turn-of-the-century buildings. The Boers besieged the city during the South African War, but many of the old buildings have been preserved. There are several other good museums and art galleries in the city. One of these is the Sol Plaatjie House, which houses displays detailing the lives of Black people during the War and in later years. Plaatjie was one of the founders of the African National Congress. The William Humphreys Art Gallery and the Duggan-Cronin Gallery contain important South African and international art works. The McGregor Museum details the cultural and natural history of the region. Underground mine tours are conducted near the Bultfontein Mine.

The Big Hole, Kimberley, was one of the richest sources of diamonds ever found

Duggan-Cronin Gallery

Egerton Rd.
Tel: (053) 833 2645.
Opening times as for the McGregor Museum but closed between 1pm–2pm Sat. Donation.

Kimberley Mine Museum and Big Hole

Tucker St.
Tel: (053) 833 1557.
Open: daily 8am–6pm. Closed: Christmas Day, Good Friday. Admission charge.

Kimberley Publicity Association

Tel: (053) 832 7298.
www.kimberley.co.za

McGregor Museum

1 Atlas St.
Tel: (053) 839 2700.
Open: Mon–Sat 9am–5pm, Sun 2pm–5pm, public holidays 10am–5pm. Admission charge.

Kimberley Mine Museum

Sol Plaatjie House

32 Angel St. Tel: (082) 804 3266.
Viewing by appointment Mon–Fri 8am–5pm.
Admission charge.

Wildebeest Kuil Rock Art Centre

Barclay West Rd.
Tel: (053) 833 7069.

The Augrabies Falls on the Orange River

Kgalagadi Transfrontier National Park

Open: Mon–Fri 10am–5pm, Sat & Sun 11am–4pm. Admission charge.
William Humphreys Art Gallery
*Cullinan Crescent. Tel: (053) 831 1724.
Open: Mon–Sat 10am–1pm & 2pm–5pm, Sun 2pm–5pm.
Admission charge.*

Near Kimberley
The battles of Magersfontein and Modder River were fought in 1899 during the South African War and its campaign to relieve Kimberley. Magersfontein was one of the worst British defeats of the war, but there were many clashes in the area, not least the Siege of Kimberley, which lasted 124 days.

There is a small museum at the Magersfontein battle site.
*The **Magersfontein battle site** is 30km (19 miles) from Kimberley on the Airport road to Modder River.
Open: daily 8am–5pm.
Closed: Christmas Day & Good Friday.*

Augrabies Falls National Park
Although they are far off the beaten track, these falls are worth visiting if travelling to the Kgalagadi Transfrontier Park. The broad Orange River dominates life in the arid Northern Cape and is the focal point of the 18,000-hectare (44,500-acre) Augrabies Falls National Park. Here the river is channelled into an 18km- (11-mile) ravine, which becomes a maelstrom of thundering white water and spray as it crashes over ledges 56m (184ft) and 35m (115ft) high. The falls are among the largest in the world. The park protects many desert and semi-desert plant species as well as antelope, including the gemsbok and springbok.

SA National Parks Central
Reservations
Tel: (012) 428 9111.
www.parks-sa.co.za

Kgalagadi Transfrontier National Park

This vast expanse of Kalahari Desert supports a surprising amount of wildlife, including lions, gemsbok, springbok, wildebeest, eland and many smaller animals. It is one of the best places in South Africa to see cheetah.

Although classified as a desert, much of the Kalahari consists of open, grass-covered plains interspersed with thorn trees and lightly vegetated sand dunes. The former Kalahari Gemsbok National Park (SA) and the Gemsbok National Park (Botswana) have been amalgamated into the Kgalagadi Transfrontier Park which is some 3.8 million hectares (9^1/$_2$ million acres) in size.

The park is 260km (160 miles) north of Upington, and distances in the park are large, so careful thought is required when planning a visit.

Many companies also offer tours to the park.

SA National Parks Central Reservations
Tel: (012) 428 9111.
www.parks-sa.co.za

Namaqualand

A vast area of the Northern Cape's huge semi-desert is a Cinderella environment. Most of the year, it is harsh and dry, but after the winter

The flowers of Namaqualand bloom in early spring

rainfall (mid-August to mid-September) it is transformed by millions of brightly coloured daisies, mesembryanthemums, aloes and other flowers. The towns of Springbok, Garies and Hondeklipbaai (Hondeklip Bay) are usually the best starting points from which to see the flowers, but it is worth checking with authorities first to find out where rain has fallen.

TRANSFRONTIER PARKS

Several transfrontier parks have been created between South Africa and its neighbours. Many of the more remote regions have declared wildlife areas on both sides of the international border. Authorities have agreed that, where possible, fences should be taken down to allow the free flow of wildlife, and tourists, across the borders. This helps create larger and more diverse wildlife areas under the joint management of the nations involved.

These include the Kgalagadi Transfrontier Park (South Africa and Botswana) and the Great Limpopo Transfrontier Park (South Africa, Zimbabwe and Mozambique). Several other transfrontier parks are being developed.

The dramatic Swartberg Pass

Springbok is also a good point from which to visit the remote Richtersveld National Park, which is botanically unusual with many rare species. The mountain desert scenery is arid, rocky and cut by jagged ravines. It is home to the semi-nomadic Nama people who have recently won back the right to graze their animals and run some tourist concessions in the park.

De Beers run tours and 4×4 trips to their rich diamond-mining concessions. These concessions are found along restricted areas of the remote windswept western coastline, which has a large population of Cape fur seals.

De Beers Diamond Coast tours
Kleinsee. Tel: (027) 807 2999.
www.debeersgroup.com

Central Karoo

The Karoo, in its various forms, extends from the Western Cape deep into the Northern Cape, Free State and Eastern Cape.

Approximately 150–300 million years ago, various deposits were laid down in the vast swamps and soggy jungles that covered the area. Today the region is rich in fossils, both of animals and plants.

Although it is an arid zone, the Karoo supports a wide range of wildlife and farming activity.

The clear and, in winter, cold skies of the Karoo make it a great place for serious astronomers and casual star watchers alike, and South Africa's largest telescope is located at Sutherland.

Karoo National Park

High mountains and wide-open plains
are part of the attraction of this 32,000-
hectare (79,000-acre) park, which
protects a wide range of animals and
birdlife. Hundreds of years ago, tens of
thousands of springbok migrated
across these plains but, these days,
numbers are far smaller, due to the
guns of countless hunters.

Karoo farmhouse

The park preserves a good cross
section of typical Karoo habitat and
supports springbok, kudu, buffalo and
smaller game. No fewer than 20 pairs of
black eagles nest in the park.

An award-winning rest camp with
Cape Dutch style cottages and
restaurant has been developed.

The nearby town of Beaufort West is
the largest in the region and the centre
of a large sheep farming community.

**South African National Parks
Central Bookings**
Tel: (012) 428 9111.
www.parks-sa.co.za

Matjiesfontein

This 19th century resort is popular with
weekenders from Cape Town. The
restored Victorian Lord Milner Hotel

Wind pump at sunset

and some other buildings in the tiny
village are national monuments. The
hotel was used as a hospital during the
South African War. The luxury Blue
Train stops here on its trip between Cape
Town and Johannesburg. The town is
260km (162 miles) from Cape Town.

Prince Albert and the Swartberg Pass

Sheltering at the foot of the Swartberg
Pass is the pretty village of Prince
Albert, which is a welcome change from
the dusty plains of the Karoo.

The steep pass climbs through the
Swartberg mountains, and the view
across the range and the plains below
are spectacular.

Prince Albert farmers take advantage
of the good water run-off from the
mountains to grow grapes and olives,
and the village has several good
restaurants. There are lovely walks and
hikes in the mountains and around the
village, and the rural atmosphere makes
a good breakaway destination.

Prince Albert Tourism Bureau
Tel: (023) 541 1366.
www.patourism.co.za

Diamonds

The discovery of diamonds marked a turning point in southern Africa's development from a rural, forgotten corner, dominated by the British Empire, to a repository of riches that in time would touch the lives of nearly everyone in the region. Diamonds are still a source of South Africa's wealth.

The first diamond discovered was the Eureka (1867), near Hopetown in the Northern Cape. Further finds occurred in 1869 on the farms Bultfontein and Dorstfontein. In 1871, fabulously rich finds were made at Colesberg Kopje, which eventually led to the development of Kimberley.

Life was probably hell for the fortune-seekers who had flocked to the site, although some of them did indeed make fortunes – and not just as prospectors.

Cut and uncut diamonds

Entrepreneurs started coaching companies, or provided such necessities as bars. The biggest headache of all was establishing ownership of this diamond-rich territory. It was called Griqualand West by the respective governments of the Free State and the South African Republic, and by the Cape Colony. It had been claimed by the Griqua, who had lived there for 70 years. In the end the British simply annexed it to the Cape (1880).

Kimberley was the cradle of the hugely profitable diamond industry that grew up in southern Africa. No-one could ever have dreamt of the riches that the Big Hole would yield. As digging continued, and the hole got deeper, squabbles broke out as miners struggled to get to their claims at ever more perilous depths.

Diamond-bearing kimberlite and gemstones

This led to the amalgamation of smaller workings, heralding the era of the big mining companies. About 20 years after the first diamond had been discovered, the De Beers mine, controlled by Cecil John Rhodes, owned virtually the entire diamond industry. Since Rhodes, and under the Oppenheimer dynasty of Ernest, Harry and now Nicky, it has become one of the world's largest and most profitable mining companies.

Diamond boats, used to collect alluvial diamonds

Western Cape

Variety is the keyword of the Western Cape. Cape Town, sheltered by the famous Table Mountain, is the gateway to this province of mountains, beaches, vineyards and a broad assortment of cultures and traditions. Both the Indian and Atlantic Oceans fringe the Cape coastline. Ranges of high, craggy fold mountains roll across the province, and in the east thick indigenous forests provide a contrast to the semi-deserts of the Karoo, which forms the northern boundary of the province.

The Western Cape's physical diversity encourages a wide variety of outdoor activity including hiking, mountain-bike riding, kloofing, paragliding, diving, surfing, fishing or good old sunbathing and swimming.

Although lacking the variety of big game that occurs elsewhere in South Africa, the Western Cape boasts a vast diversity of mammal, bird and reptile species with some unique attractions. The *fynbos* vegetation, which dominates the region, is the richest floral kingdom in the world hosting more than 7,300 species, 65 per cent of which occur nowhere else on the planet.

V & A Waterfront, with Table Mountain in the background

The bright old Cape Malay houses of the Bo Kaap

The coast also offers some of the world's best sightings of southern right whales and their newborn calves.

Closer to Cape Town, the many vineyards tempt tourists and locals alike with excellent wine and food. Throughout the region, restaurants reflect the cultural diversity of the population. Along the Cape Peninsula, small towns, including Simon's Town and Kalk Bay, have a seaside atmosphere with many good restaurants, antique shops and interesting history. Cape Town and many of the smaller centres like Darling and Hout Bay have thriving artistic communities. Theatre, music and dance performances offer a constant selection of entertainment and cultural education.

CAPE TOWN

Cape Town is a city of beaches, mountains, good food and wine, diverse culture and a laid-back view of the world. It is also a city of great contrasts, with many poor people living in sub-standard housing, as anyone driving to the airport past the thousands of shacks on the Cape Flats cannot fail to be reminded of. Whatever their economic circumstances, Capetonians pride themselves on knowing how to have fun and how to enjoy the scenic splendour that surrounds them. On weekends, the beaches and mountains attract families out for picnics and the more energetic out riding bikes, hiking, surfing and jogging.

Restaurants, ranging from the formal to the hip and trendy, cluster around

Cape Town Castle

the major beaches, the Waterfront, vineyards, and in the City Bowl itself, particularly in Kloof Street and Long Street. Cape Town is the oldest city in the country and some buildings, many of which have been restored, date back to the 17th century. Mosques, synagogues and churches attest to the many cultures that mix in the city, as do the variety of artistic styles and culinary preferences. Although many Capetonians seem to base their lives around the beaches, mountains and restaurants, the city is also home to the Houses of Parliament and several multinational corporations.

Bo Kaap Museum

This museum is in a colourful, predominantly Muslim part of Cape Town and recreates a typical 19th-century Malay home. Many of the people who live in the area are descendents of slaves. Nearby is the Auwal Mosque, one of nine in the area.

The Auwal Mosque, in Dorp Street, was built in 1798. It is recommended that visitors use one of the various companies that offer tours through this vibrant neighbourhood.

Bo Kaap Museum
71 Wale St. Tel: (021) 481 3939. Open: Mon–Sat 9am–4pm.
Admission charge.

Cape Flats townships

Gugulethu, Khayalitsha, Crossroads and Nyanga are home to the majority of Capetonians, and no visit to the region is complete without visiting these townships. Tour guides take in all the more politically significant areas and will happily stop at local restaurants or roadside cafés. All the townships are within sight of Table Mountain and make a startling contrast to the wealth concentrated on its slopes.

Many township tours also take in the Bo Kaap area and the District Six Museum.

Cape Town Tourism
Tel: (021) 426 5639/47.
www.tourismcapetown.co.za

Castle of Good Hope

Although the Castle was built as a fort in 1666–9, it has never seen battle, and the most exciting skirmishes it has overseen are those caused by the busy Cape Town traffic.

The outstanding William Fehr Collection of paintings, furniture and other items dating back to the arrival of the first white settlers is kept at the

Castle, and there is also a military museum. Tours are conducted daily (call for times), and include a visit to the dark and damp dungeon under the main castle. There are two restaurants in the castle grounds.
Buitenkant St. Tel: (021) 787 1249.
Open: daily 9am–4pm.
Admission charge.

Clifton Beach and Camps Bay

These are two of South Africa's trendiest and most image-conscious areas – fashion and money really matter here. The beaches are gleaming stretches of white sand that look like movie sets, although the water is cold. There are no shops near Clifton Beach, but vendors sell refreshments.

By day, people visit the beaches to be seen, and in the evenings the bars and restaurants of Camps Bay are packed. In summer, it is light until quite late in Cape Town (about 9pm), and Camps Bay is a good place to watch the sun set.

Company's Gardens

The paths through these gardens meander past some of Cape Town's best-known buildings, including the Houses of Parliament, St George's Cathedral, the South African National Gallery and the South African Museum. Many people merely use the gardens as a way of escaping some of the bustle of the city, and on sunny days dozens of office-workers and others sit on the lawns under the large old trees.

The Dutch East India Company established the gardens in 1652 to grow vegetables to supply their staff and passing ships. The gardens are open all day, but be cautious of 'street kids' who sometimes snatch bags or jewellery (*see box on p128*).
Upper Adderley St.

Cultural History Museum

Part of South Africa's darker history is that of slavery in the Cape. This building was first used to house slaves brought to the Cape, and in later years was used as a brothel, a post office, a jail, a library and later housed the Supreme Court. Now a museum, there are displays detailing Cape Town's history and, surprisingly, even material from ancient Greece and the Far East.
49 Adderley St.
Tel: (021) 460 8200.
Open: daily 10am–4.30pm.
Admission charge.

District Six Museum

A good example of apartheid's brutal policy of racial segregation is presented in the pictures, maps, newspaper articles and displays in this museum. District Six was a thriving community of mixed-race South Africans, until the government of the day decided they should be moved out of sight of central Cape Town, and bulldozed the entire neighbourhood.

Some of the workers at the museum used to live in the area, and each has a sad story to tell of how their homes

were destroyed. People are slowly moving back into District Six, and tours can be arranged.
25A Buitenkant St.
Tel: (021) 787 1249.
www.districtsix.co.za.
Open: Mon–Sat 9am–4pm.
Closed: Sun.

Gold of Africa Museum

This museum contains a large and unusual collection of gold masks, animals, and other artwork from all over Africa, but primarily West Africa. Goldsmiths from Ghana and Mali are particularly skilled and many examples of their work are on display.

Artefacts from Zimbabwe and elsewhere are also featured in the museum. The building which houses the museum was built in 1783.
Martin Melck House, 96 Strand St.
Tel: (021) 405 1540.
www.goldofafrica.co.za.
Open: Mon–Sat 9.30am–5pm.
Closed: Sun.
Admission charge.

Greenmarket Square

This is a good place for some casual shopping while strolling through the centre of the city. At the fleamarket, based in the cobbled square, stallholders sell a huge variety of curios, clothing and odds and ends. There are lots more formal shops in the area and restaurants.
Corner Burg St and Longmarket St.

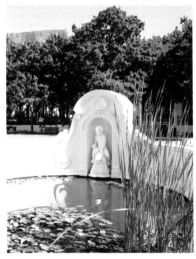
Company's Gardens

Groot Constantia

This is one of Cape Town's most elegant buildings, and is the oldest wine estate in the country. Established by Cape Governor, Simon van der Stel, in 1685, the estate has a reputation for fine red wines, but the white wines are pretty good too. Napoleon Bonaparte's time in exile on Saint Helena island in the South Atlantic was made a little easier by supplies of wine from this estate!

The Manor House Cultural Museum is well worth a visit too. There are two restaurants and, on good days, you can order a picnic and sit in the tranquil gardens to admire the wonderful views.
Groot Constantia Rd.
Tel: (021) 794 5128.
www.grootconstantia.co.za.
Open: daily 10am–5pm.
Admission charge to museum.

Houses of Parliament

During debates, parliament can be pretty noisy with vigorous heckling, but you never know when you may spot a tired MP snoozing! Tour guides help explain the workings of the South African political system and explain the history of the buildings, which were built in 1884 and opened in 1885.
Parliament St.
Tel: (021) 403 2266/403 2201.
www.parliament.gov.za.
Open: Mon–Fri. Tours on the hour from 9am–noon. Booking required.
Free admission.

Hout Bay

Although many regard Hout Bay as being a separate town from Cape Town, it is part of the greater city. The Chapman's Peak Drive offers phenomenal views across Hout Bay. Further along, as the road winds along the mountainside, there are also great views of the wide expanse of Noordhoek Beach. There is a variety of hotels and bars, including those on the Mariner's Wharf, which are good places for sundowners.
A toll is charged for vehicles using Chapman's Peak Drive.

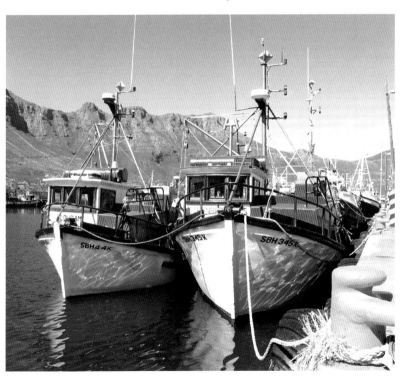

Hout Bay fishing harbour

Irma Stern Museum

Some of Irma Stern's best expressionist works are displayed here, as well as her personal collection of international art. Stern (1904–96) lived in the house for nearly 40 years, and her studio has been kept as it was when she worked there. The museum sometimes hosts exhibitions of other artists too.

Cecil Rd, Rosebank. Tel: (021) 685 5686.
www.irmastern.co.za
Open: Tue–Sat 10am–5pm.
Small admission charge.

Iziko-SA National Gallery

Some art-lovers spend a whole morning or longer at this gallery which is considered by many to be one of the best in the country. There are comprehensive displays of South African and international art from different periods including paintings, beadwork, sculptures, ceramics and textiles. Some exhibitions are changed regularly, but others are permanent.

Government Ave, Company's Gardens.
Tel: (021) 467 4660.
www.museums.org.za
Open: Tue–Sun 10am–5pm.
Admission charge, Sun free.

Kirstenbosch National Botanical Garden

A seemingly endless variety of flowers, succulents, trees and shrubs adorn the carefully tended gardens and manicured lawns that sweep up towards the steep, forested mountain slopes above. Kirstenbosch's splendid setting is alone worth the visit, but these gardens, founded in 1913, are famous among botanists worldwide for the variety of indigenous plants grown here.

There are also many rare plants of scientific and educational interest. Through careful selection, there are displays of flowers throughout the year, and in summer concerts are held in the gardens. A variety of walks ranging from short ambles to a 6km (3³/₄-mile) trail have been laid out in the 560-hectare (1,380-acre) gardens. A restaurant serves light meals and there is a shop.

Iziko-SA National Gallery

Kirstenbosch National Botanical Garden

Kirstenbosch National Botanical Garden

Tel: (021) 799 8783. www.sanbi.org
Open: Apr–Aug 8am–6pm,
Sept–Mar 8am–7pm.
Admission charge.

Long Street

Antique shops, book stores, music stores and any number of bars and restaurants line this street, which has a rather Bohemian atmosphere. The clubs may be somewhat smoky and noisy and might not be to everyone's taste, but Long Street provides an indispensable view into Cape Town's young multicultural set.

Michaelis Collection

Works by Rembrandt, Frans Hals, Jan van Goyen and other 16th and 17th century Dutch and Flemish artists such as Anthony van Dyck and Teniers form the core of this museum. Most were donated by the British-born businessman Sir Max Michaelis in 1914, and are displayed in the Old Town House. This building was built in 1755 in Cape Rococco style, and was once used as the city hall.
Greenmarket Square. Tel: (021) 481 3933. www.museums.org.za.
Open: Mon–Fri 10am–5pm,
Sat 10am–4pm.
Entrance by donation.

Pan African Market

More than 30 stallholders sell a variety of African arts from all over the continent. The market is billed as 'Africa under a roof'. People from countries as far away as Mali, Nigeria, Cameroon and Ethiopia sell their work here, and other migrants gather at the Kalukuta Republik Book Café to chat, have a meal or listen to poetry readings.
76 Long St.
Tel: (021) 426 4478.
wwwpanafrican.co.za.
Open: daily 9am–6pm.

Robben Island

'The Island', just off Cape Town, holds an almost mythical aura for many South Africans as a place of banishment and incarceration. It was here that Nelson Mandela was held for most of his 27-year imprisonment. His cell and those of other leaders are visited by thousands of people, many doing so in a form of pilgrimage to these icons.

The Quarry on Robben Island where Mandela was forced to work

Trendy Long Street

The prison has been turned into a museum explaining the role of the leaders of the liberation struggle and the brutal history of the island, which, since the 17th century, was used as a penal colony.

Much of the seashore surrounding the island is a nature reserve, and African penguins are common.
Tel: (021) 413 4200/409 5100.
www.robben-island.org.za.
Tours: Ferries leave the Nelson Mandela Gateway at V&A Waterfront 2–3 times daily. Book well in advance. Summer sunset tours at 5pm & 6pm.
Admission charge.

South African Museum and Planetarium

South Africa's oldest museum has many exhibitions displaying cultural history, wildlife, rock art and fossils. In the neighbouring planetarium, the southern skies can be explored. The museum is large and takes a while to explore.

Some of the more unusual displays are the Linton Panel containing San rock art and the Lydenburg Heads, some of the earliest African sculptures. In the Whale Well, there is, among other displays, a complete 20m- (65ft-) long skeleton of a blue whale.
25 Queen Victoria St.
Tel: (021) 481 3800.
www.museums.org.za.
Open: 10am–5pm. Closed: Christmas Day & Good Friday.
Admission charge.

Signal Hill and Lion's Head

These two landmarks provide fantastic views of central Cape Town, the Waterfront, the beaches at Camps Bay, Clifton and also Robben Island. They also help emphasise the sheer scale of Table Mountain soaring over the city.

Every day, the Noon Gun, an old cannon, is fired from Signal Hill with an explosion that is audible all over Cape Town. The tradition dates back to 1822 when the Noon Gun was used to allow ships in harbour to set their clocks accurately.

Once you have checked your watch, the nearby restaurant is a good place for a bite to eat or a drink.
Military Rd, Signal Hill.
Tel: (021) 787 1257.
Open: Mon–Sat. Free admission.

Table Mountain and cableway

'The view', wrote botanist William Burchell in 1822 after being inspired to climb Table Mountain, 'is singularly grand.' It remains so now. For just under four centuries the 1,087m- (3,566ft-) high mountain has been the

Table Mountain cableway

TABLE MOUNTAIN NATIONAL PARK

Nearly every mountain between Table Mountain and Cape Point, a distance of some 60km (37 miles), falls into this park (formerly Cape Peninsula National Park). The park is the richest botanical area for its size on earth, and a variety of mammals, birds and fish are also protected. It is an unusual national park in that it falls entirely within a metropolitan area. There are hundreds of kilometres of hiking trails along the mountains and beaches, although there is limited accommodation within the park and at Cape Point. Most people merely stay in urban areas and walk straight onto beaches or the mountainsides.
Tel: (021) 701 8692.
www.tmnp.co.za

Thunder City jets

focal point of Cape Town, influencing weather patterns and even people's attitudes. It forms a bold northern front of a high range stretching 60km (37 miles) to Cape Point. The mountain's slopes and ravines offer dozens of walks and climbs from the easy to the severe, while the cable car transports passengers to the summit's viewing platforms and restaurants.
Cable station.
Tel: (021) 424 8181.
www.tablemountain.net.
Opening hours vary according to season. Also check weather conditions as the cable station may close in bad weather.

Thunder City

Thunder City is one of the few places in the world tourists can go for a flip in a combat jet but, be warned, the flights are for the rich only. Even if you can't afford a

sub-sonic flight over the Cape peninsula, the aircraft and other memorabilia can be viewed at close range when they are not flying. Thunder City has an English Electric Lightning, BAe Buccaneer and Hawker Hunter on display.
Cape Town International Airport.
Tel: (021) 934 8007.
www.thundercity.com.
Open: Mon–Sun 9am–5pm.
Admission charge.

Two Oceans Aquarium

Spending time at the Two Oceans is bit like taking a fantastic scuba-diving trip without getting wet. Shoals of deep-sea fish, sharks, rays, coral reef displays, turtles, seals and penguins all provide hours of education and entertainment. For those who are prepared to get wet, there are interactive displays where children can touch some sea creatures, and qualified divers can even arrange to swim in the tank where the sharks live.

The aquarium is home to fish and marine life from both the South Africa's warm east coast and the cold west coast waters.

Dock Rd, V&A Waterfront.
Tel: (021) 418 3823.
www.aquarium.co.za.
Open: daily 9.30am–6pm. Feeding times, daily: 11.30am and 2.30pm (penguins). Predators: 3pm. Seals: 11am and 2pm. Admission charge.

Two Oceans Aquarium

Victoria and Alfred Waterfront (V&A Waterfront)

Once disused harbour land, the Waterfront is a vast collection of hugely popular shops, curio stores, restaurants, cinemas and museums. Many of the restaurants overlook the harbour, and in good weather the walkways and piers fill up with people enjoying a drink or a meal, while watching activity in the working harbour.

Several hotels are part of the complex. Ferries leave from here for Robben Island and sunset cruises along the coast.

Open: daily.

The Victoria and Alfred Waterfront

Tour: The Cape Peninsula

The Cape Peninsula's mountain chain curves south from Cape Town, dips at Constantia Nek, rises at Constantiaberg, falls away over Silvermine to the Fish Hoek Valley, then swings past Simon's Town to the southeast. For 12km (7 1/2 miles), before finally tumbling into the sea at Cape Point, it blends into the unspoiled wilderness of the Cape of Good Hope Nature Reserve (now part of the Table Mountain National Park).

Allow one day. In the centre of Cape Town, take Somerset Road at its junction with Buitengracht Street and continue along Main Road through Sea Point to the M6.

1 The Atlantic seaboard

Sea Point's Promenade is a favourite stretch for slow walks or faster jogs. Further on, at Bantry Bay, little

Saunders Rock Beach with its tidal pool offers safe bathing.

Beyond, Clifton has the country's most fashionable beaches. Next door, Camps Bay's beaches are sprawled dramatically at the foot of the magnificent Twelve Apostles. The road winds on past Bakoven to Llandudno, picturesquely climbing up steep slopes, with Sandy Bay, a nudist beach beyond. *The M6 climbs the hill above Llandudno, then descends towards Hout Bay.*

2 Hout Bay

Wood (*hout*) was obtained here for early Cape Town buildings. The town has a lovely beach, waterfront development and a fishing harbour, which is the centre of the snoek industry and base of the crayfishing fleet. The World of Birds bird sanctuary is in the Hout Bay Valley.

Simon's Town on the Peninsula

CAPE TOWN

Table Bay

Mouille Pt

Green Point

Sea Point

Bantry Bay

Clifton

Camps Bay

Bakoven

Woodstock

N1

N7

Langa

Lavistown

N2

Mowbray

1087m
▲
Table Mtn

Rondebosch

Claremont

Athlone

Guguletu

Nyanga

M6

Twelve Apostles

M3

Bishops Court

Kenilworth

Llandudno

World of Birds

Sandy Bay

Constantia

Groot Constantia
Manor House

Plumstead

Philippi

Hout Bay

Dieprivier

Grassy Park

Rondevlei

M3

Tokai

Retreat

Strandfontein

592m ▲
Chapman's Peak

Lakeside

Chapman's Point

Noordhoek

Silvermine
Nature Res

Muizenberg

St James

Kalk Bay

M65

Clovelly

Fish Hoek

False Bay

Kommetjie

Glencairn

Simon's Town

The Boulders

Scarborough

M4

Miller's Point

M65

Cape of Good Hope
Nature Reserve

**Smitswinkel
Flats**

CAPE POINT

N

0   5   10km

Cape of Good Hope

Cape Point

Return to the M6, and follow the signs to Chapman's Peak.

3 Chapman's Peak

The 10km (6-mile) drive around Chapman's Peak to Noordhoek is one of the world's most spectacular scenic passes, with exceptional views across the bay. It gives access to excellent climbs and mountain walks.

From Noordhoek, follow the M6 from which, after the first traffic lights, the M65 branches right to Kommetjie.

4 Noordhoek and Kommetjie

Noordhoek's lovely 6km (3³/₄ miles) Long Beach is favoured by horseback riders. At its end, Kommetjie is a quiet village with a popular surfing beach. A shallow tidal pool provides safe bathing for children.

From Kommetjie, the M65 continues through Scarborough to the Cape of Good Hope.

5 Cape of Good Hope Nature Reserve

This magnificent 7,750-hectare (19,150-acre) nature reserve is now included in the Table Mountain National Park. It straddles the Peninsula's tip and is home to mountain zebra, bontebok, eland and baboons.

There are drives and places to picnic and swim. The view from Cape Point across False Bay, so called because it was often mistaken for Table Bay, is spectacular.

Tel: (021) 780 9204.
www.sanparks.org
Open: daily.
Admission charge.

At the exit, turn right if you want to visit the southern tip, then return north, turning right on to the M4 to Simon's Town.

6 False Bay

The approach to Simon's Town is via The Boulders, where the swimming, among huge boulders, is shared with a colony of African penguins. Simon's Town, South Africa's largest naval base, is a quaint seaside town, beyond which is Fish Hoek – a popular resort with wide, safe beaches.

The dramatic False Bay coast

Kalk Bay, with antique, junk and craft shops, is home to the False Bay fishing fleet. Beyond, St James has a small beach with a tidal pool. Alongside it, Muizenberg's magnificent beach offers safe bathing. Visit the Natale Labia Museum and Rhodes Cottage memorial museum.

Continue on the M4 past Lakeside, and follow the signs to the M3 and the city.

Simon's Town Museum
Court Rd. Tel: (021) 786 3046.
www.simonstown.com

Open: Mon–Fri 9am–4pm, Sat 10am–1pm, Sun 11am–3pm.
Admission charge.

Natale Labia Museum
192 Main Rd, Muizenberg.
Tel: (021) 788 4106/7.
www.iziko.org.za
Open: Mon–Sat.
Admission charge.

Rhodes Cottage
Main Rd, Muizenberg.
Tel: (021) 788 1816.
Open: 9am–4pm.
Donation.

Hout Bay from Chapman's Peak

Whale watching

The southern Cape is one of the best places in the world for land-based whale watching. Every year, between June and November, large numbers of southern right whales are spotted all along the coastline.

The whales migrate from the cold southern oceans to the warmer coastal waters to give birth and mate, before beginning the long journey south to their primary feeding grounds again. They are often seen close inshore with their calves, which measure about 5m (16^1/2ft) at birth.

Humpback whales are also often spotted, although in smaller numbers and usually further north along the KwaZulu-Natal coast as they migrate to their calving and mating grounds near Madagascar. Both species of whales tend to gather in small groups.

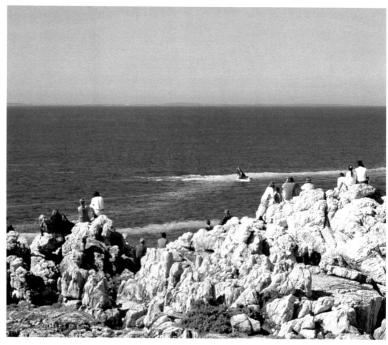

Whale watching

The largest number of southern right whales usually congregate between False Bay and Hermanus, where the sea cliffs make ideal viewing platforms from which to watch them.

The whales sometimes 'breach', lifting most of their bodies out of the water, before crashing in again with a huge splash. They also 'sail' with their heads underwater and their tail flukes protruding into the air. Humpbacks display more regularly and in even more spectacular fashion. It is believed that these displays are part of courtship and other social rituals.

Both species of whale were hunted heavily in the past. The southern right whale is so called because it floats when killed, and was considered the 'right' whale to hunt, but since hunting restrictions were imposed, their numbers have begun increasing fairly quickly.

The whale-watching industry has boomed in recent years, particularly around Hermanus, and several companies specialise in both land- and boat-based whale watching. The boats are strictly regulated, and it is illegal to approach the whales too closely.

There are a wide variety of B&Bs and hotels in the area, as well as good restaurants. The area is busy in whale-watching season, which usually reaches its peak in September and October.

Many other species of whale occur in South African waters, as do twelve species of dolphin. Common, bottlenose, dusky and humpbacked dolphins are often seen along the coast. Near Sodwana Bay on the KwaZulu-Natal coast, swimmers often mingle with dolphins near shallow reefs.

Southern right whales

The southern right whale grows to a maximum length of 15–17m (49–55ft) and weighs 50–65 tonnes (49–64 tons). They are not deep divers and seldom stay submerged for more than 20 minutes. They eat small crustaceans (krill) found relatively close to the surface. Little is known of their social structure, but the mothers form very strong bonds with their calves.

Humpback whales

These whales grow to about 14m (45ft) in length and feed on small crustaceans (krill) and small fish. They weigh between 25–40 tonnes ($24^{1}/_{2}$–39 tons).

Humpback whales are well known for their 'songs' a series of squeaks, moans and whistles of varying pitch, which can last up to 30 minutes. They usually stay submerged for a fairly short time, seldom longer than 15 minutes.

Winemaking

The South African wine industry has grown by leaps and bounds in recent years and has developed a considerable export market. There are hundreds of small boutique vineyards scattered throughout the Western Cape, cheekily rubbing shoulders with the big well-established vineyards.

Franschhoek, Stellenbosch and Paarl are the best-known South African wine-producing regions, but clever winemakers in towns like Worcester, Robertson and Montagu, some 180km (110 miles) from Cape Town, have now leapt into the market. Wealthy business people and foreigners who vie with each other to hire the best and most innovative winemakers have bought numerous vineyards.

Winemaking and fruit-growing provide economic sustenance for entire valleys in the Western Cape. Even people not directly involved in the cellars earn their livelihoods from associated businesses like restaurants, craft shops, cheese-making and tourism.

Many vineyards offer wine-tasting tours and others run good restaurants on their properties too. Each region – all in all there are 17 recognised wine routes – offers organised tours, although many tourists opt to drive themselves and spend a few days in the scenic winelands.

Whitewashed, gabled houses, surrounded by vines sheltering in valleys beneath high fold mountains, make for picturesque touring conditions ideal for enjoying good wine and food.

All the regions offer other activities, including horse riding and hiking, and trout, yellowfish and bass fishing. There are a wide range of B&Bs, guest farms and lodges throughout the winelands.

Although experts consider South African red wines to be superior to the whites, many new winemaking techniques and cultivars have been

Grapevines

developed to make the most of local conditions. Cabernet Sauvignon, Shiraz and Merlot are the most common reds, although the local Pinotage cultivars are also popular. There is a large range of whites with Chardonnay, Chenin Blanc and Sauvignon Blanc being the choice of many cellars.

South Africa's winemaking history dates back some 350 years, and the first vineyards were planted in 1655. South Africa also makes excellent sherry and fortified wines (better known as port, although European Union trade regulations forbid the use of the more familiar name).

Some vineyards can trace their origins back to the arrival of the French Huguenots in the 17th century. Brandy is also produced in some areas, and there is even a brandy-tasting route.

It is well worth buying one of the many wine guides on offer. One of the best is John Platter's *Guide to the Wines of South Africa*.

Vineyards near Darling

Elsewhere in the Western Cape

There are dozens of beautiful places within easy reach of Cape Town. The best known are the winelands which stretch inland from the city boundaries through Stellenbosch, Franshhoek and Paarl and then along the east coast to Walker Bay. There are good beaches all along the coast between Cape Town and the Garden Route and mountain ranges cut through the entire region. Many pretty villages and towns are also within easy reach of Cape Town.

Franschhoek

The beautiful Franschhoek Valley is one of South Africa's premier wine-producing areas, and has become an extremely fashionable place to live and to holiday.

In 1688, the Cape Governor, Simon van der Stel, granted French Huguenot refugees land in the valley which earned the area its name meaning 'French Corner'.

Today most estates in the valley offer wine-tasting, and many have excellent restaurants. The region caters specifically for tourists, and there are many art and curio shops as well as

Franschhoek vineyard

delicatessens offering local products. There are many scenic drives through the valley, and it is also worth visiting the Huguenot Museum.

Franschhoek Wine Valley Tourist Association
Tel: (021) 876 3603.
www. franschhoek.org.za

Stellenbosch

Stellenbosch is perhaps the town most often associated with South African wine, and was founded by Dutch Governor Simon van der Stel in 1679. The town, its culture and its economy revolve around the wine industry and the University of Stellenbosch.

There are many fine examples of Cape Dutch architecture, with some of the best examples in Dorp, Church and Drostdy streets. There is a variety of museums for those tired of tasting wine and eating good food in the surrounding vineyards.

Stellenbosch Tourism Bureau
Tel: (021) 883 3584.
www.stellenbosch.org.za

Paarl

Paarl (The Pearl) is another important wine-growing centre and, although it does not share the charm of Stellenbosch or Franschhoek, the wines are no less delicious.

Stellenbosch

Paarl vineyards

Although the town was established in the early 18th century, the area had been settled and farmed since the late 1600s. Despite the focus on wine farming, other agriculture is also important. There are pleasant walks in the nearby Paarl Mountain Nature Reserve.

Paarl Tourism Bureau
Tel: (021) 863 4937
www.paarlonline.com

Langebaan

The Langebaan Lagoon forms part of the West Coast National Park, and is an internationally important birding wetland. Whales are sometimes spotted from the shore, and in August and September there are usually good showings of wild flowers. The nearby village of Langebaan is a useful stopover when visiting the Park, which is some 100km (60 miles) north of Cape Town.

Some 46km (29 miles) north of Langebaan is the small fishing village of Paternoster, which is well known for its crayfish and other seafood. Many people stopover for weekend lunches and to photograph the whitewashed fishermen's villages.

The nearby Columbine Nature Reserve protects a variety of coastal plants and wetland birds.

Langebaan Tourism Bureau
Tel: (022) 772 1515.
www.langebaaninfo.com

Ceres

This town can only be reached by one of three scenic mountain passes, and is one of South Africa's premier deciduous-fruit growing areas.

Ceres is named after the Roman goddess of fruitfulness, and has a good climate with more than 230 days of sunshine a year on average.

STREET KIDS

'Street kids' are homeless youngsters who live on the streets of South Africa's larger cities. Many abuse drugs, and in particular sniff glue. Sadly, some of these children resort to crime as a means of surviving. They usually work in groups with one child distracting the victim as the others snatch bags, necklaces or any other item they can grab. Many also beg at traffic lights.

It is best to resist giving them money, because it is often used to buy glue. There are several organisations and shelters that try to offer these children better lives.

Kite surfing in Langebaan

Kite surfing in Langebaan

Various tours of fruit farms can be undertaken, as well as visits to nearby game reserves, San rock art sites, hikes, mountain biking and fishing. The town is about an hour and forty minutes drive from Cape Town.

Ceres Tourism
Tel: (023) 316 1287.
www.ceres.org.za

Cederberg Wilderness Area

The 162,000-hectare (400,296-acre) wilderness area covers the rugged peaks and valleys, which provide good hiking and a huge variety of plant life. The towns of Citrusdal and Clanwilliam make good bases from which to explore the mountains and surrounding farms. After good rains, many flowers cover the *veld*, although they are not usually as prolific as those further north in Namaqualand (*see Northern Cape, pp98–103*). The area is about 220km (137 miles) north of Cape Town.

Elsewhere in the Western Cape

Stall near Ceres

Oudtshoorn humour – ostriches don't fly and you can't make cheese from them

Cape Nature Conservation
Tel: (021) 426 0723 for hiking permits.
www.capenature.org.za
Citrusdal Tourism Bureau
Tel: (022) 921 3210.
Clanwilliam Tourism Bureau
Tel: (027) 482 2361.
www.clanwilliam.info

Tulbagh
Church Street in Tulbagh has no fewer than 32 national monuments – all classical Cape Dutch buildings, with whitewashed walls and thatched roofs, dating back as far as 1754. Most of the cottages were severely damaged or destroyed in a rare earthquake in 1969, but were all lovingly restored to their former glory.

The Oude Kerk Volksmuseum contains displays telling the story of the earthquake and the restoration project. The De Oude Drostdy Museum, which was built in 1804, is a fine example of Cape Dutch architecture.

The area also has many wine estates, restaurants and B&Bs. The more energetic can take horseback or bicycle rides through the pretty valley, or undertake hikes of varying strenuousness.

Tulbagh Tourism Bureau
Tel: (023) 230 1348.
www.tulbaghtourism.org.za

Cape Agulhas/Arniston
Cape Agulhas is Africa's most southerly tip, despite the commonly held belief that it is Cape Point. Nearby, the

Ostrich eggs in Oudtshoorn

Tulbach is packed with pretty Cape Dutch houses

Swartberg Pass

Oudtshoorn and the Cango Caves

Oudtshoorn used to be the ostrich feather capital of the world, and exported tons of these once-popular fashion items to Europe in the late 19th and early 20th centuries. Even now, ostriches are widely farmed, but these days meat and leather are more important products than feathers, although many farms put on ostrich shows and races. Tourists can also ride on the ungainly creatures, the largest of the world's birds.

Many Victorian and older buildings line the streets of the town. The chambers and stalactites and stalagmites of the Cango Caves lure tourists underground some 32km (20 miles) north of Oudtshoorn. An hour-long guided tour takes visitors through the large main caves, but the system runs much deeper under the Swartberg mountains.

Oudtshoorn Tourism Bureau
Tel: (044) 279 2532.
www.oudtshoorninfo.com

thatched-roofed and white-walled houses of Arniston have been declared national monuments, and white, windswept beaches have a harsh beauty.

Cape Agulhas is about 100km (60 miles) south of Swellendam. On the way, the Shipwreck Museum at Bredasdorp has a display of artefacts collected from the many ships wrecked along this coast.

The nearby De Hoop Nature Reserve offers protection to a wide array of vegetation, mammals and sealife. The marine reserve along the shoreline extends 5km (3 miles) out to sea. Whales are often spotted here, usually from August to October.

Witsand Tourism
Tel: (028) 537 1010.
www.witsand.com

CAPE MOUNTAIN PASSES

Dozens of steep mountain passes with magnificent scenery are a feature of the Western Cape and the Garden Route. A whole range of skilfully designed roads cut from the coast through the fold mountains to the interior. Further inland, the passes are no less spectacular, and many are worth travelling through merely for the scenery. Some of the better known are the Swartberg Pass near Prince Albert, the Du Toits Kloof Pass (use the old main road) between Paarl and Worcester, the Prince Alfred Pass near Knysna, the Franschhoek Pass and the Outeniqua Pass near George.

Cango Caves

Tel: (044) 272 7410. www.cangocaves.co.za. Open: daily. 9am–4pm. Admission charge and guided tours.

Swellendam

South Africa's third-oldest town is built on the slopes of the Langeberg mountains and close to the wide Breede River – scenery that complements the whitewashed walls of the town's many old buildings.

The town was established in 1743 and soon after, in 1746, the building which now houses the Drostdy Museum, was constructed. The museum incorporates several other nearby buildings with displays of period furniture, clothing and art. The Dutch Reformed Church, although only built in 1911, includes Baroque, Gothic and eastern architecture.

The nearby Marloth Nature Reserve has a network of hiking trails through the mountains.

Swellendam Tourism Bureau

Tel: (028) 514 2770.
www.swellendamtourism.co.za

Drostdy Museum

Tel: (028) 514 1138. Open: daily.
www.drostdymusuem.com

Bontebok National Park

The beautiful bontebok antelope has prospered in this national park, which is South Africa's smallest. The antelope was hunted to the verge of extinction, and this park has played an important role in the recovery of the bontebok, which only occurs in the Western Cape. Cape mountain zebras and a variety of smaller antelope, birds and reptiles also occur here. The reserve protects an important area of shrub *fynbos*, which has been ploughed up for wheat fields elsewhere in the region.

The park is close to Swellendam.
Bookings: **SA National Parks Central Reservations.** *Tel: (012) 428 9111. www.sanparks.org*

Elsewhere in the Western Cape

Drostdy Museum, Swellendam

Tour: The Garden Route

The Garden Route is one of South Africa's most scenic drives. Skirting the Indian Ocean, and occasionally dipping inland through lush nature reserves, forest, high mountain passes and lakes, this is a coast of holiday-towns and resorts. The Knysna and Tsitsikamma regions are covered in dense indigenous forest, and in places steep cliffs drop directly into the sea. Accommodation is plentiful, and activities range from hiking and walking to water sports and golf. The region is very busy at Christmas and Easter.

Allow at least three days. Start in George.

1 George and the Wilderness National Park

The high, forested Outeniqua Mountains form the backdrop to George, one of the biggest towns on the Garden Route. The internationally renowned Erinvale Golf Course is on the outskirts of town. Founded in 1811, George has various museums and buildings of interest including the Outeniqua Railway Museum.

The Wilderness National Park just east of George protects a series of coastal lakes that form an important refuge for water birds.

Outeniqua Railway Museum and Outeniqua Choo-Tjoe

Tel: (044) 382 1361.
Museum open: Mon–Sat 8am–5pm.
Call to confirm times as the schedule sometimes changes.
Continue along the N2 for 62km (38 miles) to Knysna.

2 Knysna and the Swartberg Pass

Built around the huge, scenic Knysna Lagoon, this town has grown into one of South Africa's most popular tourist resorts.

Knysna Heads

Tsitsikamma National Park

Open to the sea between high sandstone cliffs called The Heads, the lagoon is an important nursery for fish and other sealife, and is also used for a wide variety of watersports. There are many good beaches near Knysna including Noetzie (10km/6 miles south), which has a luxurious lodge built in the form of a castle and broad secluded beaches surrounded by forest. The best beaches are located around 10–15km (6–10 miles) west of the town.

Nearby, the exceptionally scenic Swartberg Pass climbs through South Africa's largest patch of indigenous high forest – some 36,000 hectares (89,000 acres) containing yellowwood and stinkwood trees.

Knysna Tourism. www.knysna-info.co.za.
Continue along the N2 to Plettenberg Bay.

3 Plettenberg Bay and Robberg Peninsula

'Plett' is one of South Africa's most fashionable beach resorts. The long, broad, gently curved beach attracts many sun-worshippers at Christmas, but out of season it is quiet. The Robberg Peninsula, which is part of the Robberg Nature and Marine Reserve juts out into the sea south of the town

Plettenberg Bay

and offers pleasant walks and broad vistas. Nearby, Keurbooms River also has good beaches and a river estuary.
Continue along the N2 to the Tsitsikamma National Park.

4 Tsitsikamma National Park

Running for about 80km (50 miles) along the coast, and 5km (3 miles) out to sea, the park is a spectacular ribbon of forest deeply incised by rivers that have cut their way through the mountains to the sea. The indigenous

forest still has some examples of huge yellowwood trees, and a variety of hikes and walks meander through the forest.

The 5-day Otter Trail hike takes in the area in all its splendour, as the path follows the coast along high cliffs and through the forest and river crossings.

Otter Trail bookings can be made through South African National Parks Central Reservations, and need to be made as long as a year in advance. *Tel: (012) 248 9111. www.sanparks.org*

Knysna waterfront

Lesotho and Swaziland

Although these tiny nations are both independent, their tourism industries are closely linked to South Africa. Most tourists visiting these countries will usually have travelled to South Africa first. Both countries are poor and predominantly rural. Swaziland has a pleasant climate, although parts can be hot in summer, and Lesotho is very mountainous and cold in winter. Swaziland has several good hiking trails and game reserves. The highlands of Lesotho are well suited to pony trekking.

Lesotho

The high Maluti and Drakensberg mountains dominate most of this tiny kingdom's scenery. Life among the rugged mountains is harsh, and heavy snowfalls with temperatures way below freezing are common in winter. Many of the mountain peaks are higher than 2,500m (8,200ft), and no point of the country is lower than 1,000m (3,300ft) above sea level.

A Basotho man with his traditional hat and blanket

Several companies run pony trekking operations and guided hikes. 4×4 trips across the mountains are also available. The horse, or more specifically Basotho pony (a small, stocky, shaggy-coated horse), is the primary source of transport for many people in the mountains. Although crops are grown at lower levels, most people living at high altitude depend on sheep, goats and, to a lesser degree, cattle herding for a living.

Lesotho is entirely surrounded by South Africa, and most of its citizens earn their livelihoods there. The capital city of Maseru has some interesting craft stores, but the real beauty of the country lies in the mountains, waterfalls and deep valleys.
www.seelesotho.com

Swaziland

This small, predominantly rural kingdom is sandwiched between South Africa's eastern border and

Mozambique. Many Swazis have relatives living in South Africa on whom they are economically dependent. Even so, Swaziland has a distinct cultural identity that sets it apart from its much larger neighbour.

The Milwane Game Reserve, set in the fertile Ezulweni Valley, offers good game viewing and horse riding. Further north, the hills of Malalotja Nature Reserve are an excellent hiking destination. The Ezulweni valley has several hotels, golf courses and craft and art shops.

The capital Mbabane is 360km (224 miles) from Johannesburg by road. The border is open from 6am–9pm. Some nationalities require visas. *www.welcometoswaziland.com*

Swazi crafts on sale near Mbabane

Swazi women in traditional dress

Shopping

South Africa has a huge variety of goods to tempt both the casual souvenir-hunters and serious shoppers. Prices vary: shopping malls and high streets, particularly those in tourist areas, tend to be the most expensive, market stalls less so and roadside vendors the cheapest. But, just as the prices vary, so does quality, and shoppers should be cautious when buying at the roadside. Market and roadside vendors expect to bargain, but shop owners in upmarket malls are less flexible and seldom oblige with lower prices.

WHERE TO SHOP
Antiques

Antiques have risen in price in recent years, but many dealers sell quality products that may tempt collectors of Africana and knowledgeable buyers.
For a list of the shops, phone the **South African Antique Dealers' Association** *Tel: (011) 880 2387.*
www.saada.co.za

West African masks for sale at the Rosebank African Market

Curios and carvings

A wide range of wooden masks, carved animals, wooden headrests, beadwork and weaving from all over Africa are sold at markets and by roadside vendors. The quality of some of these products is extremely good, and knowledgeable buyers should be able to make reasonable buys.

Many of these products are sold by migrants from elsewhere in Africa, and chatting with them about their travels can be an interesting experience. Some people take weeks to get to South Africa, travelling by bus or truck with their goods.

Be cautious when buying pottery, carvings and other wooden products at the roadside or at markets. Examine the carvings for cracks that are sometimes disguised with wood filler or shoe polish. Try to establish whether pottery or ceramic items have been properly fired, especially when shopping in rural areas.

Gemstones and jewellery

Many South African dealers sell top-quality gems and jewellery, and tourists benefit from a VAT (14 per cent) rebate on leaving the country. The jeweller will assist you with the paperwork. This rebate only applies in shops accredited to the Jewellery Council of South Africa.

Jewellery Council of South Africa
Tel: (011) 807 4681.
www.jewellery.org.za

Wild animal products

Various wild animal products, including trophies, skins, leather belts and shoes are sold at markets and in shops. Whatever one's view on buying these products, it should be remembered that many countries have strict rules concerning the importation of animal products. It is also illegal to sell ivory and some other animal products, including the skin of the African rock python.

Should you be offered ivory or any other animal product you suspect to be illegal, it is best to notify the police or conservation authorities. Youngsters at the side of the road commonly sell tortoises, but this trade is illegal and should be reported.

Wine

Nearly all cellars are willing to ship wine overseas. Local wines are usually a

Part of the Spier Wine Cellar range

Addy Hoyle Gallery, Clarens

good buy in comparison with international prices. Wine dealers will also be able to advise on customs limitations on quantities that may be imported to various countries.

BOOKS AND MAPS

Exclusive Books and **CNA** stores have branches throughout the country. *See telephone directory.*

Cape Town
Clarke's Bookshop
Rare and second-hand books, prints and maps, books on South Africa.
277 Long St, 8001.
Tel: (021) 423 5739.
www.clarkesbooks.co.za

Durban
Adams & Co
341 West St. Tel: (031) 304 8571.
www.adamsbooks.co.za

Johannesburg
Collectable Books
Antiquarian books, maps, prints and Africana. Also small oils and watercolours.
No 6 The Village, 80 Tyrone Ave, Parkview. Tel: (011) 646 8320.

CURIOS, ARTS AND CRAFTS
Cape Town
Heartworks
South African ceramics, beadwork and other items for the home.
98 Kloof St. Tel: (021) 424 8419.

Clarens
Addy Hoyle
Art gallery, mainly local paintings of landscapes, fantasy birds, animals and other works.
Clarens, Free State. Tel: (058) 256 1832.
www.addyhoyle.co.za

Durban
Africa Art Gallery
Painting, sculptures and other works by some of South Africa's best artists.
7 Chartwell Centre, Umhlanga Rocks.
Tel: (031) 561 2661.
www.africaartgallery.co.za

Selling carpets at Kingdom Weavers in Balgowan, KwaZulu-Natal

Johannesburg
Art Africa
Ethnic arts and collectables from many parts of sub-Saharan Africa.
62 Tyrone Ave, Parkview.
Tel: (011) 486 2052.

Kim Sacks Gallery and School of Ceramics
Selection of art, jewellery and ceramics.
153 Jan Smuts Ave, Parkwood.
Tel: (011) 447 5804.

KwaZulu-Natal Midlands
Kingdom Weavers
African rugs, tapestries and other items.
Curry's Post, Balgowan.
Tel: (033) 234 4205.

JEWELLERY AND GEMSTONES
Cape Town
Olga Jewellery Design Studio
Skilfully designed jewellery of all types which can be made to personal preferences.
Victoria Wharf. Tel: (021) 419 8016.

Johannesburg
Charles Grieg
100-year-old family business at the forefront of South African jewellery.
Shop U25, Sandton City.
Tel: (011) 783 3174.

MARKETS
Many cities, towns and villages hold markets on weekends. Check with local tourist authorities for locations and times.

Cape Town
Green Point Fleamarket
Everything and anything from art and clothes to cheese and biltong.
Green Point Stadium. Open: Sun & some public holidays, weather permitting.

Johannesburg
Newtown Market Africa
Cosmopolitan Saturday hub. Antique African costume, masks, junk, beads.
Newtown Cultural Precinct. Open: Sat 9am–4pm.

Durban
Amphitheatre Market
Fleamarket with over 700 stalls.
North Beach. Open: Sun.

Al fresco dining

OUTDOOR EQUIPMENT
Cape Town
Cape Union Mart
Gear for camping, climbing and hiking.
Victoria Wharf, The Waterfront. Tel: toll free 0800 034 000. Branches nationwide.

Surf Centre
Beach and casual clothing, wetsuits and the like. Primarily women's wear, but has men's section.
454 Canal Walk Centre, Century City, Milnerton. Tel: (021) 555 4970.

Johannesburg
Cape Union Mart International
Everything for the outdoors from pocketknives to sleeping bags.
Hyde Park Shopping Mall. Tel: (011) 325 5038. Branches nationwide.

Outdoor Warehouse
Tents, camping, hiking equipment and everything for life outdoors.
8 Tungsten St, Strijdom Park, Randburg. Tel: (011) 792 8331. Several branches elsewhere.

SHOPPING MALLS
Cape Town
Cavendish Square
High-quality shopping, cinemas, restaurants.
Dreyer St, Claremont. Tel: (021) 657 5600. www.cavendish.co.za

Colourful curio shops on the Garden Route

Durban
Gateway Theatre of Shopping
Shopping, leisure and entertainment under one roof. Also extreme sports facilities.
Durban North. Tel: (031) 566 2332.
www.gatewayworld.co.za

Johannesburg
Rosebank Mall
Fashionable shopping, cinemas, restaurants and fleamarkets on Sundays. The Zone opposite the Mall is a trendy hangout for teenagers.

Pretoria
Menlyn Park Shopping Centre
Same attractions as most other centres, but with a rooftop drive in.
Menlyn, Pretoria.
Tel: (011) 348 8766.
www.menlynpark.com

The Zone in Rosebank

Entertainment

Entertainment in South Africa is eclectic and mirrors the broad range of cultures and traditions of the country's people. Music and theatre often take on cross-cultural flavours, although Shakespeare and more traditionally Western plays are firm favourites in some circles. The Government has taken to heart the development of the performing arts, and the Department of Arts, Culture, Science and Technology actively promotes development of theatre, music and other disciplines. Cultural officers work throughout the country to encourage youngsters, and to assist existing groups to improve their skills in the performing arts.

BALLET AND DANCE

Traditional ballets are regularly performed in the larger centres, but less commonly so in smaller towns and rural areas. Highly talented local dancers perform in most productions, and an increasing number of international companies and dancers are visiting South Africa.

Dance takes on many forms in South Africa, and ranges from traditional Zulu and Venda dances that have been performed for centuries to various forms of modern dance, tap and classical. The best traditional dancing is often performed at cultural villages in rural parts of the country where cultural links to the past are often stronger than those in the cosmopolitan cities. At many of these performances the performers will explain the significance of each dance and what role it plays in society. Some dances are performed only at weddings, others are linked to seasonal festivals and some are just for fun.

Traditional dance is also often incorporated into music performances with band members and vocalists joining in. Ballroom dancing is extremely popular, particularly in townships. Children and adults get togged up in formal suits and dresses and compete for national awards.

THEATRE

As with music, theatre in South Africa reflects the diversity of the population. A Chekhov play may be running at one theatre while a John Kani production is on at the next, and some other theatre work that falls into no particular camp will also attract audiences.

Much of South Africa's modern theatre has drawn on the experiences of the political struggle, although many playwrights are now exploring new themes.

Booking tickets

Most theatre, opera, ballet and cinema tickets can be bought through Computicket, which has offices nationwide.
Open: Mon–Fri 9am–5pm, Sat 9am–4pm. Cash or credit card. They also handle online and telephonic booking. Nationwide call centre. Tel: (083) 915 8000 or (011) 340 1000. Tel: (083) 131 for information.
www.computicket.com
(Many sports match tickets can also be booked through Computicket.)

Cape Town
Artscape Theatre Centre
Theatre, ballet, opera, classical music.
DF Malan St, Foreshore.
Tel: (021) 410 9801.
www.artscape.co.za

The Baxter Theatre Centre
A Cape Town institution. Theatre, ballet, classical music.
Main Rd, Rondebosch.
Tel: (021) 685 7880.
www.baxter.co.za

Independent Armchair Theatre
Hosts an unusual array of comedy and other entertainment, often by young and upcoming performers.
135 Main Rd, Observatory.
Tel: (021) 447 1514.

Theatre on the Bay
Relaxed theatre, and you can take your drinks in with you.
1 Link St, Camps Bay.
Tel: (021) 438 3301.
www.theatreonthebay.co.za

Darling
Evita se Perron
Pieter-Dirk Uys, South Africa's foremost satirist.
Darling Station, Arcadia Rd. (Darling is about an hour's drive north of Cape Town.)
Tel. (022) 492 2851.
www.evita.co.za

Durban
The Playhouse Theatre
A Durban favourite. Theatre, classical music and other shows performed in three venues.
Smith St, opposite City Hall.
Tel: (031) 369 9555.

Evita se Perron Theatre, Darling

Johannesburg

African Bank Market Theatre

A theatre with a proud history of hosting politically sensitive plays and supporting Black actors.
Newtown Precinct. Tel: (011) 832 1641.
www.markettheatre.co.za

Johannesburg Civic Theatre

Comprises three theatres: large, middle-sized and small.
Loveday St, Braamfontein.
Tel: (011) 877 6800.
www.showbusiness.co.za

Liberty Theatre on the Square

Small comfortable theatre.
Nelson Mandela Sq, Sandton.
Tel: (011) 883 8606.

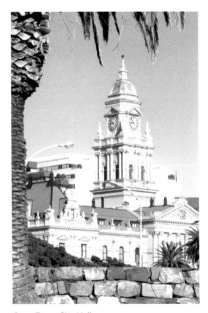

Cape Town City Hall

Pretoria

State Theatre Complex

Theatre, classical music and opera in several venues.
320 Pretoria St, Pretoria.
Tel: (012) 392 4000.
www.statetheatre.co.za

CINEMA

The South African film industry is developing in leaps and bounds, and many international studios are using South Africa as a filming location. Most large centres hold regular film festivals, details of which are usually listed in local newspapers and on tourism authority websites.

Ster-Kinekor and Nu Metro, the two largest distributors of films in South Africa, have screens all over the country, mostly in shopping malls. Local newspapers publish movie listings. Some cinemas are not part of the major commercial networks and often show films not distributed on circuit.

Drive-in cinemas can still be found in some areas. The Top Star in Johannesburg is positioned on the top of a huge mine dump and has views right across the city.

Ster-Kinekor
Tel: (082) 167 89. www.sterkinekor.com
Nu Metro
Tel: (086) 110 0220. www.numetro.co.za

Cape Town

Imax

Amazing large-format screen, usually showing spectacular wildlife events.

Victoria and Alfred Waterfront.
Tel: (021) 419 7365. www.imax.co.za

The Iziko-SA National Gallery

Sometimes shows documentaries and films by local independent filmmakers. Check their listings sheets.
Government Ave.
Tel: (021) 456 1628.

The Labia

A favourite Cape Town venue. Fashionably laid-back, with a bar downstairs.
68 Orange St, Gardens.
Tel: (021) 424 5927.
www.labia.co.za

Durban

Watch newspaper listings for shows at museums.

Johannesburg

Cinema Nouveau (9 cinemas)
Shows a variety of limited release and alternative films.
The Mall of Rosebank.
Tel: (011) 445 7000.

MUSIC

Whatever your taste in music you should be able to find it in South Africa, and there might even be something completely new. South African music is increasingly influenced by the music of Africa, particularly West and Central Africa, and any number of bands and performers can be found experimenting with new trends.

Jazz, blues, and reggae are hugely popular amongst the majority of the population. The younger generation favour *kwaito* (the South African form of rap), trance, house and general pop. There are also a variety of venues that play good old-fashioned rock and roll. Check the local paper to see what's on. Occasionally rock concerts featuring international and local stars are hosted at sports stadiums or indoor arenas.

Opera and classic music are often performed in the larger cities, sometimes in the grand old buildings built as city halls. Theatre and opera-goers usually dress fairly smartly but leave their best clothes for opening nights. In clubs people wear whatever they feel like or whatever they think their friends think they should wear!

Cape Town

Cape Town City Hall

Classical music and opera in grand surroundings.
Darling St.
Tel: (021) 410 9809. www.cpo.org.za

Green Dolphin

Live jazz and dining.
V&A Waterfront. Tel: (021) 421 7471.
www.greendolphin.co.za
Open: all week.

Mannenberg's Jazz Café

Live jazz and dining. Music usually from 8.30pm.
Clock Towers Centre, V&A Waterfront.
Tel: (021) 421 5639. Open: all week.

Durban
Catalina Theatre
Operettas, classic music.
Wilsons Wharf. Tel: (031) 305 6889.
www.catalinatheatre.co

Durban City Hall
Home of the KZN Philharmonic
Orchestra. Classical music and other
concerts.
Smith St. Tel. (031) 369 9438.
www.kznpo.co.za

Johannesburg
Johannesburg City Hall
Classical music and other performances.
President St.
Johannesburg Computicket.
Tel. (011) 789 2733.

Thousands flock to the summer evening
concerts at the Kirstenbosch National
Botanical Gardens

Kilimanjaro
Very trendy supper-dance club.
Melrose Arch, Melrose.
Tel. (011) 214 4300.

Kippies Jazz International
Famous Johannesburg jazz club.
Market Theatre Complex.
Tel. (011) 836 1805.
www.kippies.co.za

Linder Auditorium
Classical music and theatre.
Wits Education Campus,
St Andrews Rd, Parktown.
Tel: (011) 643 6413.
Bookings through Computicket.

OPEN-AIR VENUES
Cape Town
Kirstenbosch Summer Sunset
Concerts: jazz, classical music,
choirs. Winter: visitor centre hosts
concerts.
Kirstenbosch National Botanical
Gardens, Rhodes Dr, Newlands.
Tel: (021) 799 8783. www.nbi.ac.za

Oude Libertas Amphitheatre
Classical music and dance.
Adam Tas Rd, Stellenbosch.
Tel: (021) 809 7380.
www.oudelibertas.co.za

Durban
Botanical Gardens
Sometimes hosts outdoors concerts.
Tel: (031) 201 1303.
Sydenham Rd, Musgrave.

Johannesburg
Walter Sisulu National Botanical Gardens
Popular classical music in the gardens on summer afternoons.
Malcolm Rd, Poortview, Roodepoort. Open: 8am–5pm all year. Admission charge.
Tel: (011) 958 1750 or 958 0529.
www.nbi.ac.za

BARS AND PUBS
As is to be expected in a place like South Africa, there are a huge number of bars and pubs. Nearly all offer food and drink, but in a sports-mad country it's the establishments that screen live sports matches that get really packed.

In these pubs and bars, most of the important international rugby, cricket and soccer matches are screened live, and the atmosphere in the better venues is second only to being at the game. The partisan fans welcome anyone who enjoys sport.

Golf, Formula One racing and English soccer are also regularly screened, as are special events including the Olympics and the Tour de France. The more seriously sports-oriented pubs show the matches on big screens.

Cape Town
The Fireman's Arms
Fun 1906 vintage bar with great atmosphere.
25 Mechau St, City Bowl.
Tel: (021) 419 1513.

The Sports Café
Screens endless international sport.
Upper Level, Victoria Wharf.
Tel: (021) 419 5558.

Durban
Billy the Bum's
A venue favoured by a generally young and affluent crowd.
504 Windermere Rd.
Tel: (031) 303 1988.

Johannesburg
Billy the Bum's
Owned by the same group as the Durban pub. Similar crowd, same sports.
Pineslopes Centre, Witkoppen Rd.
Tel: (011) 465 2621.

The Grand Slam
A huge venue that gets packed with hundreds of people during important games.
Corner Witkoppen Rd and Sycamore Dr.
Tel: (011) 454 3700.

Listings
Check local daily newspapers for listings sections. The national *Mail&Guardian* newspaper, published Fridays, gives excellent coverage to major cities. The *Mail&Guardian* also has a very good entertainment section on its website: *www.mg.co.za*

Most regional tourism websites have links to 'what's on', in their areas.

Sport and leisure

South Africans love sport, and many people spend their weekends either participating in games or watching matches live or on television. Football is by far the most popular sport, but cricket, rugby, golf and other games all have their fans. South Africa's good climate and varied geography also encourage watersports and adventure activities. Surfing, diving and boating have large followings, and in recent years adrenaline junkies have taken to skydiving, whitewater rafting, shark diving and other exciting pastimes.

Sports bodies and venues

South Africa has world-class sporting facilities, and the cricket, rugby, soccer and athletics stadiums compare with the best. Most provinces have world-class golf courses.

A comprehensive list of all the sporting bodies in South Africa can be found on the website of **Sport and Recreation South Africa**.

Tel: (012) 304 5137. www.srsa.gov.za. The website includes contact numbers, scheduled meetings or matches, officials and venues. It is particularly good for helping plan which events to attend.

Contact details for major sports:

Athletics South Africa
Tel: (011) 880 5800.
www.athletics.org.za

Cricket South Africa
Tel: (011) 880 2810.
www.cricket.co.za

South Africa has some great surfing spots

GOLF

An increasing number of tourists are taking advantage of good weather and cheap rates to play on South Africa's championship-standard golf courses. Many exclusive housing estates have been constructed recently around courses designed by golfing legends Gary Player and Jack Nicklaus, amongst others.

The Fancourt Country Estate near George on the Garden Route, the Gary Player Country Club at Sun City and The Pecanwood Estate near Pretoria are among the best, but there are good courses in many other parts of the country. Most accept visitors.

Regional tourism authorities and hotels will have details of how to book a round or look at: www.golfinginsouthafrica.co.za.

South African fast bowler Makhaya Ntini

Cycling South Africa
www.pedalpower.co.za

The Horse Society of Gauteng
Tel: (011) 702 1657. www.thsinfo.co.za

Motorsport South Africa
Tel: (011) 466 2440.
www.motorsport.co.za

South African Football Association
Tel: (011) 494 3522.
www.safa.net

South African Golf Association
Tel: (011) 783 5474.
www.saga.co.za

South African Rugby Football Union
Tel: (021) 659 6900.
www.sarugby.net

THE BIG EVENTS

Some of the most important events on South Africa's sporting calendar attract tens of thousands of participants and are among the biggest of their kind anywhere. More than 14,000 athletes participate in the annual Comrades Marathon raced over 89km (55 miles) between Durban and Pietermaritzburg. Held on 16th June, it is regarded by many as one of the world's premier 'ultra-marathons'.

The Argus Cycle race is one of the largest in the world. Every year in April, some 34,000 cyclists follow the spectacularly scenic 106km (66 miles) course that treats participants to stunning views of the mountains, sea and beaches.

The Midmar Mile in KwaZulu Natal is another 'en masse' sporting event where thousands of swimmers race across the Midmar Dam.

South African sport

When Bafana Bafana ('The Boys'), South Africa's football team, loses a match, the event immediately sparks radio talk show discussions, letters to newspapers and heated debate in bars, on buses and on street corners. Fire the coach! Fire the administrators! Ask the government to intervene!

South Africans don't like losing, and the response is similar if the national rugby team does badly at the World Cup or the cricket team does not meet expectations. Most sporting nations are passionate about their favourite team, but in South Africa losses and victories take on a special edge because sport here often has a political sub-plot.

For decades Black players were barred from participating in top teams, and sports administrators are still trying to ensure that equal opportunities are offered to all in terms of training, facilities and financial backing.

Long-denied international competition because of sports boycotts imposed in protest against apartheid, sports fans are eager for success, and woe betide the teams that don't fulfil these aspirations. At the top end, sports stadiums and facilities are world class, and the nation has hosted the Rugby World Cup, Cricket World Cup, Africa Cup of Nations (soccer), the Africa Games (athletics) and several internationally important golf tournaments during the last ten years.

Football is by far South Africa's most popular sport. Across the nation, television and, particularly in poorer and rural areas, radio, keep millions up to date on important matches, both local and international. As is the case with football matches anywhere, attending a big match is a raucous affair and fans, some in fancy dress, whistle and blow bugles to urge on their team.

Many teams have imaginative names, and the Dangerous Darkies (humourously named if politically incorrect), usually get thrashed by Kaiser Chiefs, the country's most popular team. Kaiser Chiefs have a

Fancourt Golf Course, near George, Garden Route

Football supporters

fan club that stretches far into Africa, and a game against arch-rivals Orlando Pirates (both teams are based in Soweto) is one of the highlights of the season and is treated with the same frenzy as a World Cup Final.

Rugby fans are no less passionate, and the national team has a hundred-year-old reputation of being one of the toughest and best in the world, a reputation that is sometimes hard to live up to in the demanding world of professional sport.

Traditionally dominated by White Afrikaans speakers, rugby is changing its profile to be more representative. One of its defining moments was Nelson Mandela holding the World Cup with victorious captain, Francois Pienaar, in 1995.

Cricket is another sport in which South Africa has excelled and a sport that is also changing its racial profile to become more representative. Athletics and boxing are also popular, and South Africans have performed well on the international stage. Many athletes participate in the professional athletic circuits in Europe and Asia.

The country's long-distance **runners** are particularly successful, and a large number of marathons are organised every year. South Africans have consistently been listed among the world's top golfers, although the sport has fairly limited appeal because of the cost of playing the game regularly.

As befits a country with lots of sunshine, **watersports** are widespread. Many people water-ski on inland lakes and dams on weekends, much to the annoyance of others participating in the far more leisurely, but hugely popular, fishing. Popular **ball sports** include basketball, field hockey, bowls, netball and tennis. South Africans also enjoy **gambling**, and most large cities host regular horse race meetings.

FOOTBALL WORLD CUP

South Africa will host the 2010 Football World Cup, one of the world's most popular sporting events.

The tournament attracts hundreds of thousands of fans, and is expected to provide a huge boost to the South African economy with a simultaneous increase in other forms of tourism. The country has many excellent football and rugby stadiums (which are often also used for football matches) and others will be renovated to cope with the expected influx of visitors.

Football is the most popular sport in Africa where South Africa's hosting of the Cup is regarded as particularly prestigious.

Children

South Africa's good climate and open spaces make it a pleasant place for children to visit. In the cities, many teenagers hang out in shopping malls where they can go to see films, chat with their friends or get something to eat in safety. In many cases the 'kids culture' is very American, and Hollywood films, television, pop stars and even fast food often have an American orientation.

Travelling with small children

All the essentials from disposable nappies to DVDs are widely available. Bear in mind that if you are travelling, distances between locations can be very long, so carry books and games. Many South African parents resort to allowing their children to play endless mobile-phone games to ease the boredom.

There are excellent service stations on most major routes, and these have well-looked-after toilets, fast-food outlets and shops. Some even have small gardens where children can use up surplus energy.

Many South African fast food and family restaurants have children's menus.

Playing in the sea at Camps Bay

Swimming

Currents along the South African coast can be powerful and unpredictable. Never allow children to swim unattended. Many more popular beaches have lifeguards, but the coastline is long, and it is not possible to patrol it all. Some beaches have tidal pools that make for safe swimming. Make sure that children refresh their sun block regularly.

National parks

All the national parks are well equipped to cater for children, and many rest

Walter Sisulu National Botanical Gardens

camps have playgrounds and swimming pools. All the camps at the major parks are fenced and are quite safe. Do not let children, or anyone else, feed the monkeys or baboons.

In some of the larger parks, hyaenas have learnt that some people throw supper scraps over the fence and make nightly patrols to see what food has been left out. Do not feed them and don't let children go up to the fence with food in their hands. Hyaenas have immensely powerful jaws.

Not all private game lodges allow children under the age of 16 or, in some cases, 14.

Hotels

Some hotels can arrange a babysitting service. Both local and satellite TV services have a selection of children's programmes.

There are a wide range of entertainment parks, playgrounds and children-orientated activities available in most cities and towns. Many special activities and entertainments are organised over the Christmas and Easter holidays. Tourism authorities will be only too happy to tell you what has been arranged in their area.

Kleinmond Estuary, Western Cape

Food and drink

South Africans are just as fond of local dishes as they are of Italian, Chinese, Indian and other cuisines from around the globe. South Africa is generally one of the world's more carnivorous countries, and there are very few dedicated eating places for vegetarians; that said, some restaurants will have at least one vegetarian choice on the menu. Most people will find something that suits their preferred diet. Meat features prominently in many meals, but although it is cheap by Western standards, it is regarded as a luxury by poor people. Chicken is extremely popular as an affordable form of protein.

South African specialities

Biltong

Biltong is more than a snack food for many South Africans; it's almost a cult item. Connoisseurs will debate the fat content of the spices and the moisture content. It's like wine tasting for beer-drinking sports fans.

Biltong, savoury dried meat, is sold all over South Africa. It is eaten while having a drink in a bar, watching a rugby match on television or pretty much at anytime someone feels like a salty snack. It is usually made from beef or game animals, including kudu and eland. Ostrich meat is also used.

Strips of raw meat are usually dipped in vinegar, coated in ground coriander seed, black pepper and salt and then hung in a cool dry place to cure. Under the right circumstances, it is ready after a few days and is cut into thin slices. The early Dutch settlers originally used the recipe as a means of preserving meat.

Bobotie

Bobotie is ground lamb flavoured with turmeric, cinnamon and other spices covered with a form of custard and baked in the oven. It is usually served with yellow rice, raisins and stewed fruits.

Boerewors

This is a homemade sausage filled with a variety of meats and spices. *Boerewors* (farmers' sausage) is a favourite among many South Africans.

Bunny chow

Bunny chow is a Durban phenomenon. A half loaf of square-shaped bread is hollowed out and filled with meat or vegetables. The inside of the bread is used to scoop the curry out.

Cuisine from around the world is popular with diners across South Africa

THE BRAAI

In simple terms, a *braai* is a barbecue where meat, poultry, fish or vegetables, or all of them, are grilled over an open fire.

The *braai* is a whole cultural experience that is popular in all sectors of the population. As with the '*potjie*' everyone has their own idea as to the perfect recipe and method, but in the end the *braai* serves the same purpose for all – it's a great way to socialise, relax and enjoy good weather. Beer, wine and other drinks usually accompany the event.

You will find South Africans having a *braai* in the lush gardens of Camps Bay in Cape Town, the dusty streets of Mhlabathini in Zululand or in the rest camps at the Kruger National Park. Almost everyone '*braais*'.

Koeksisters

Koeksisters are favourites among Afrikaans-speaking people, and are made from fried dough dipped in very sweet syrup.

Mealies

Mealies (maize on the cob) roasted over an open brazier are a popular snack food for many South Africans. They can often be bought on city street corners particularly in Johannesburg, Soweto and surrounding areas. They are usually quite crisp and chewy.

Mopane worms

Mopane worms are an acquired, peppery taste, but worth a try. *Mopane* worms are the caterpillar of the emperor moth and are dried in the sun. They are very nutritious and are eaten as a snack or with *pap*. They are often sold on the streets of Johannesburg, Pretoria and Pholokwane and are sometimes served in restaurants that specialise in African food.

Pap en vleis

Pap en vleis (firm porridge and meat) is the favourite food of many South Africans. The meat is usually barbecued or grilled and the '*pap*' is a firm porridge made from de-husked maize and served with gravy. *Pap* is as popular amongst Zulu- and Xhosa-speaking people as it is in Afrikaans-speaking communities. In various forms it is found throughout southern and east Africa. In Zulu it is called *phutu*, amongst Zimbabweans it is *sadza* and in parts of Zambia it is called *ntshima* – in short, most people eat it. Some people prefer it moist, some dry; others like it with sour milk and others with gravy.

Potjiekos

Potjiekos is meat and vegetables cooked in a heavy cast-iron three-legged pot. The pot (*potjie*) is placed over open coals and the stew is left to simmer for hours. Everyone has their own recipe and method and will stoutly defend their way of cooking a *potjie* (pronounced 'poyt-key') as being the only way to do so.

Prawns peri-peri

Prawns *peri-peri* is a recipe brought to South Africa by Portuguese visitors from Mozambique. Prawns are coated in olive oil, lemon juice, garlic and *peri-*

peri (hot ground chillies), and then grilled.

Sosaties
Sosaties (kebabs) are skewered lamb, beef or even vegetables.

Smoorsnoek
Smoorsnoek is a typical Cape Malay dish made with smoked snoek (a large predatory fish similar to a barracuda), chilli, onions, potatoes and sometimes tomato. It is usually served with some form of chutney or jam, and the snoek should be smoked over oak.

Waterblommetjie breedie
Waterblommetjie breedie (water lily stew) is a form of stew made from lamb and the buds of indigenous water lily.

WHERE TO EAT AND DRINK
Price guide:

★ = main course up to R65

★★ = up to R85

★★★ = over R85

Cape Town
Blues★★

Trendy seafood restaurant right over the road from Camps Bay Beach.

South Africa's good weather is ideal for outdoor festivals and fairs

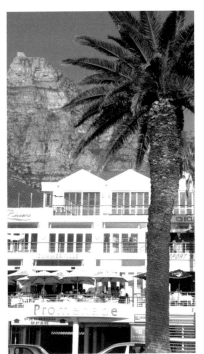

Cape restauranteurs make the most of the wonderful scenery and great location

Victoria Rd, Camps Bay.
Tel: (021) 438 2040.

Buitenverwagting★★★
Old favourite on lovely wine farm. Great place to spend an afternoon or for dinner.
Klein Constantia Rd, Constantia.
Tel: (021) 794 3522.

Cape Colony★★★
Top-class, refined restaurant with formal menu and excellent service.
Mount Nelson Hotel, Gardens.
Tel: (021) 483 1198.

Cape to Cuba★★
Friendly and fun, with a view of the harbour. Good seafood and old Havana décor.
Main Rd, Kalk Bay.
Tel: (021) 788 1566.

Durban
Florida Road
A variety of cafes and bars on this busy street are good places for a cocktail or drink.
Florida Rd, Durban.

The Havana Grill★★
Lively grill house with excellent meat and seafood dishes.
Shop U2, Suncoast Casino.
Tel: (031) 337 1305.

Royal Hotel★−★★★
Several busy bars.
Smith St, opposite City Hall.
Tel: (031) 333 6000.

Franschhoek
Le Quartier Francais★★
Lovely alfresco dining, but warm inside in winter. Skilfully run with a top-class reputation.
Main Rd, Franschhoek.
Tel: (021) 876 3105.

Johannesburg
Gramadoelas★★
The best-established traditional South African food restaurant in Johannesburg. Also dishes from elsewhere.

Market Theatre, Newtown.
Tel: (011) 838 6960.

The Grill House★★
Top-class steak, lamb and seafood.
Try Katzy's next door for a late-
night drink.
32a Cradock Ave, inside Rosebank Mall.
Tel: (011) 880 3945.

Kapitan's Café★
Wonderful curries and atmosphere
in a restaurant once frequented by
Nelson Mandela.
1a Kort St. Tel: (011) 834 8048.
Daytime only.

The Turtle Creek Winery★★
Great for a drink under the oak trees in
summer and sit in front of a lovely fire
inside in winter.
12 Wierda Valley Rd.
Tel: (011) 884 0465.

Yum★★★
One of the top restaurants in the
country – choose from designer
salmon, calamari and rump steak.
Relaxed atmosphere.
12 Gleneagles Rd, Greenside.
Tel: (011) 486 1645.
www.yum.co.za

Knysna
The Oystercatcher★
Oysters fresh from the sea and a great
view of the lagoon.
Small Craft Harbour, Knysna.
Tel: (044) 382 6943.

Pretoria
La Madeleine★★★
Top-class Mediterranean-style
restaurant, popular with politicians.
122 Priory Rd, Lynwood Ridge.
Tel: (012) 361 3667.

Stellenbosch
Spier Estate★★★
Cape Malay buffet and other meals on a
wine state with lovely gardens. Café too.
Baden Powell Dr, near Stellenbosch.
Tel: (021) 809 1100.

Tulbagh
Paddagang Wine House★
Traditional Cape menu includes
smoked snoek pate.
23 Church St, Tulbagh.
Tel: (023) 230 0242.

EATING OUT

Restaurants in South Africa are similar to
those found throughout the western world,
but it must be remembered that there are
strict anti-smoking laws that allow smoking
in designated areas only. Most restaurants,
particularly more expensive establishments,
enforce these laws.

Nearly all good restaurants, excluding a
few which are *Halal*, serve alcohol. If you
intend taking your own wine, it is worth
checking beforehand about corkage charges,
because in some instances these are high.

If any item on the menu is marked SQ, ask
the price before ordering – these dishes tend
to be expensive.

If you intend visiting a restaurant and the
weather is good, which is often, even in
winter, ask about outside seating – many
South Africans take good weather for granted
and forget to mention outside eating areas.

Food and drink

Eating in South Africa

Whisky, cocktails, or even beer – you can usually find your favourite tipple in most South African bars

Only a few dishes are truly indigenous to South Africa, and the country's culinary tradition is derived from the cuisine of a variety of countries. Many recipes have been adapted over the centuries with the inclusion of local ingredients and the introduction of innovative cooking methods.

Indigenous cuisine

Maize forms the staple diet of the vast majority of South Africans. It is usually prepared in the form of *pap*, a stiff porridge made from ground de-husked maize.

It is served with meat or vegetables, but in poorer homes meat is something of a treat. *Pap* is also eaten with *maas* (milk curds).

Samp (whole de-husked maize) and kidney beans is another popular dish. Sorghum, a cereal indigenous to Africa, sweet potatoes, onions, pumpkins and a variety of wild plants are also commonly used. Wild spinach is used to make a stew called *morogo*, which is often spiced with a chilli-based relish.

Many restaurants in the townships serve these meals regularly, and more and more upmarket restaurants specialising in African foods are creating stylised versions.

Other cuisines

Many South African dishes have their origins elsewhere in the world. Dutch, English, Indian and Malay people have all contributed to the style and flavour. The Malay slaves who worked in the kitchens of Dutch settlers helped introduce Indonesian sweet and sour dishes, pickles and chutney.

The Indian population in KwaZulu-

Natal brought curries, samosas and nan bread with them, and some English-speaking South Africans still enjoy a Sunday lunch of roast beef complete with Yorkshire pudding.

Many of the dishes have been adapted over time and have become truly South African products.

Restaurants

South Africa has an enormous variety of restaurants offering international cuisine from around the globe. Italian, Indian, Portuguese, Greek, Chinese and Japanese food is widely available. French cuisine is also popular, particularly in restaurants based in the winelands.

Johannesburg has a growing Chinese population and, in the Bruma area, there are more Chinese restaurants than any other.

Meat forms the basis of many meals among those who can afford it.

Top South African chefs are highly skilled and produce world-class food

There are any number of grill houses that prepare excellent steaks, rack of lamb or pork spare ribs. Fresh seafood is usually available in seafood restaurants along the coast and in Johannesburg, where restaurateurs have fresh fish, oysters, crayfish (a species of rock lobster) and prawns flown in regularly.

Several restaurants specialise in venison, and springbok, eland and kudu are often available, as well as game birds including guinea fowl. Most restaurants cater for vegetarians, but some with more skill than others. Of course there are any number of fast-food outlets serving burgers, chicken or fish in forms familiar all over the world.

Drink

The country's favourite alcoholic drink is beer, most of which is drunk in the form of bottled lager, but traditional sorghum beer, or *mahewu*, is also hugely popular.

Wine is widely available, and many South Africans pride themselves on their knowledge of the local industry.

In KwaZulu-Natal, cane spirits is a popular addition to cola, and brandy is a favourite in Limpopo and the Western Cape. For the bold there is *mampoer* or *witblits*, which has a very high alcohol content and is made of just about anything, but usually grains or fruit. Treat with caution!

Hotels and accommodation

South Africa has a wide choice of places to stay, ranging from luxury resort and city hotels to backpackers hostels, campsites, lodges on private game reserves and bed-and-breakfast guesthouses. Standards are generally high and good accommodation can be found even in smaller towns. Local tourist offices are happy to help visitors find accommodation of all kinds and to suit all budgets.

If arriving at your destination without prebooked accommodation, your best bet is to visit the local tourist office. For the absolute cream of places to stay, Classic Retreats

Rooms with a view of the pool at Arniston Hotel

(*www.classicretreats.com*; tel: + 27 (11) 234 1026, or in the UK: (0131) 661 6000) has an unrivalled portfolio of gorgeous town house hotels, country lodges and private game reserves throughout South Africa.

The Three Cities group (*www.threecities.co.za*) is South Africa's leading hotel group, with more than 30 luxury city and resort hotels, game lodges and country house hotels strategically located in all the country's most-visited areas. The South African Automobile Association (*www.aatravel.co.za*) is the largest online database for accommodation in hotels, B & Bs, guest houses, self-catering chalets and apartments, lodges and game reserves throughout South Africa.

Budget accommodation

There are backpackers' lodges in most of the bigger cities and along the most popular tourist trails such as the Garden Route. These offer dorm rooms and some may also offer double or twin rooms, with shared bathroom and cooking facilities.

Camping and caravanning

Most game reserves have campsites with shared ablution blocks and outdoor cooking facilities. There are also campsites at most popular beach and surf resorts, with space for motor homes as well as tents. Several companies rent camper vans. Camping or staying in a camper van overnight is not advisable except in a secure campsite.

Hotels

Hotels are rated from one to five stars but the rating system is voluntary and some hotels and B&Bs choose not to be rated. There are world-class luxury hotels in all major cities and in most resort areas, and there are also numerous smaller 'boutique hotels' in many cities and smaller towns.

National parks

Comfortable chalets with self-catering facilities are standard in most national parks and game reserves. Not all have en-suite facilities, but all are usually spotlessly clean.

Private game lodges

Private game lodges – usually on the fringes of national parks such as Kruger – also offer luxury accommodation in the wild, along with guided game drives. Two- and three-star hotels are generally also comfortable.

JOHANNESBURG
Hilton Sandton★★★

With 329 bedrooms, the Hilton combines the best of business and leisure facilities within secure landscaped grounds.
138 Rivonia Rd, Sandton.
Tel: (011) 322 1888.
www.hilton.com

DURBAN
Quarters Hotel★★★

A gorgeous, 24-room townhouse hotel made by converting four Victorian homes in Durban's trendiest suburb.
101 Florida Rd, Morningside, Durban.
Tel: (031) 303 5246.
quarters@icon.co.za

KRUGER NATIONAL PARK
Lukimbi Safari Lodge★★★

Located on 15,000 hectares (37,100 acres) of unspoilt wilderness, this marvellous safari lodge offers Big Five game viewing from open-top vehicles and is perfect for families, as it has child minders and a children's programme.
Kruger National Park. Tel: (011) 888 3713. www.lukimbi.com

LIMPOPO
Makweti Safari Lodge★★★

In Limpopo's pristine, malaria-free Welgevonden Private Reserve, this superb lodge offers wilderness luxury. Welgevonden Game Reserve.
Tel: (011) 837 6776.
www.makweki.com

Hotels and accommodation

CAPE TOWN

Boulders Beach Lodge★

Cheap and cheerful, friendly
guesthouse within hopping distance of
the African penguin colony at Boulders,
some of whose members are regular
visitors. Comfortable cottage-style
rooms, excellent restaurant, great value
for penguin lovers.
Boulders Beach Lodge, Boulders,
Simon's Town.
Tel: (021) 786 1758.

Cape Grace Hotel★★★

This elegant hotel is the perfect base for
first arrivals to Cape Town and is the
best address on the lively V&A
Waterfront. All 122 rooms have superb
views of the harbour, Table Mountain
(or both) and are full of personalised
touches. Intimate atmosphere, stylish
design and a great restaurant add to its
appeal. Highly recommended.
West Quay Rd, Victoria & Alfred
Waterfront.
Tel: (021) 410 7100.
www.capegrace.com

Cape Milner Hotel★★

Highly acclaimed city hotel in the
trendy Tamboerskloof district, with
chic atmosphere, boutique-hotel
ambience and rooftop pool.
24 Milner Rd, Tamboerskloof.
Tel: 0861 000 333 or (021) 426 1101.
www.capemilner.com

Lagoon Beach Hotel★★

On a huge stretch of sandy beach at
Milnerton, a ten-minute taxi ride from

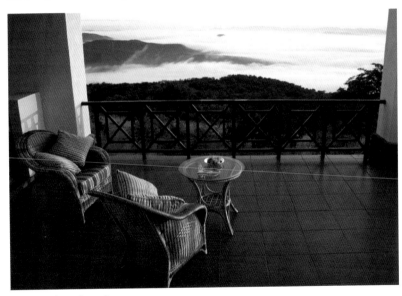

Pakamisa Private Game Reserve

downtown Cape Town, the Lagoon
Beach has an excellent restaurant, two
pools, modernistic rooms and very
helpful staff. An excellent compromise
between beach and city.
Lagoon Beach Rd, Milnerton.
Tel: (021) 528 2000.
www.lagoonbeachhotel.co.za

WINELANDS & KAROO
Blaauwbosch Private Game Reserve★★★
This luxury private game reserve with
its extensive domain and game is the
perfect way to experience the African
wild on a visit from Cape Town. Very
comfortable rooms, swimming pool,
dining room and bar, dazzling starlit
African skies.
Blaubosch, Karoo.
Tel: (049) 835 9099.
www.blauwbosch.co.za

Mardouw★★
Superb family-owned, very
professionally managed, country-club-
style hotel with extensive grounds, golf
course, pool, rose garden, and a range
of extremely comfortable
accommodation.
*Between Ashton and Swellendam on
R60, 26 km (16 miles) from Swellendam,
20 km (12 miles) from Ashton.*
Tel: (023) 616 2999.
www.mardouw.com

River Bend★★★
Country-house style comfort in lovely
suites with shared pool and excellent
restaurant and bar on a private reserve

adjoining the malaria-free Addo
National Elephant Park.
Addo Elephant National Park.
Tel: (042) 233 8000.
www.riverbendlodge.co.za

River Manor Country House and Spa★★
It's worth visiting Stellenbosch just to
stay in this gracious home from home,
with 16 spacious and prettily furnished
en-suite rooms in two historical Cape
Dutch houses loaded with charm – as
are your hosts and their team. Two
pools, pretty garden, the bars and
restaurants of downtown Stellenbosch
less than five minutes' walk away and an
exclusive health and beauty spa as well.
The Avenue, Stellenbosch.
Tel: (021) 887 9944.
www.rivermanor.co.za

GARDEN ROUTE
Arniston Hotel★★
The best hotel on Arniston's seafront,
with the colourful harbour and quaint
old fishing village right next door. The
exterior is plain, the rooms are bright,
breezy and well appointed, and there is
a pool, a gourmet restaurant and a
more casual restaurant-bar. The ocean
view is unbeatable.
126 Beach Road, Arniston, Bredasdorp.
Tel: (028) 445 9633.
www.arnistonhotel.com

Kurland★★★
It is impossible to over-praise this
absolutely idyllic manor house estate,

with rooms set in thatched houses on a huge estate famed for its polo horses. An open-air pool is surrounded by wooded gardens, rooms are huge and bathrooms are sybaritic. Excellent breakfast and dinner. Fast internet access.
The Crags, Plettenberg Bay.
Tel: (044) 534 8082.
www.kurland.co.za

Mitchell Street Village★★

Tucked away on a quiet street five minutes from the centre of Hermanus, this is an impressive and friendly boutique guesthouse with unexpectedly upscale facilities including minibars in all rooms, two pools, and pretty gardens. Highly recommended.

56–60 Mitchell Street, Hermanus.
Tel: (028) 312 4560.
www.56.co.za

Pezula★★

Perched on a prime location on Knysna's Eastern Head, the Pezula Resort Hotel & Spa is South Africa's most luxurious resort hotel, with breathtaking views complemented by gourmet cuisine, lavish suites, a superb spa, championship golf course and vast range of outdoor activities. Friendly staff and outstanding personalised service.
Eastern Head, Knysna.
Tel: (044) 302 3410.
www.pezula.com

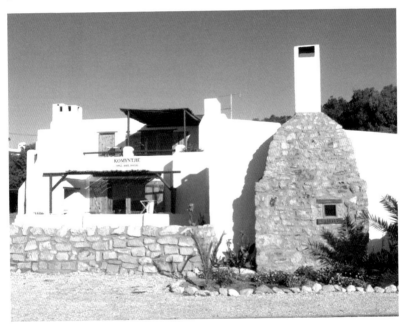

Self-catering accommodation in Paternoster

Language

South Africa has no fewer than 11 official languages, but most people manage to communicate through a combination of Zulu, English or Afrikaans. South Africans are multilingual and speak five languages regularly. Most people in South African business and tourism communicate in English. Signage is also in English. Major newspapers are in English, Afrikaans and Zulu.

Place names

Throughout South Africa, many geographical names are in Afrikaans, Zulu, Sotho and other local languages. Many of the Afrikaans names make reference to animals or natural phenomenon, such as snow or the colour of rocks. A lot of the names are an interesting, if rather sad, record of the former distribution of wild animals, many of which were hunted to the point of local extinction. Since the 1994 elections, the names of some landmarks that formerly had Afrikaans names have been replaced with ones from Black languages. Pietersburg, originally named after a Voortrekker leader, is now called Polokwane after a local chief. Some Zulu place names are prefixed with *kwa* which means 'place of', as in Kwambonambi ('place of the Bonambi clan'). *Kwa* is often used as a prefix to the names of rivers, mountains or plains.

Common terms

English: Yes	**Afrikaans:** Ja	**English:** Good morning	**Afrikaans:** Goeie more
Xhosa: Ewe	**Zulu:** Yebo	**Xhosa:** Molo	**Zulu:** Sawubona
English: No	**Afrikaans:** Nee	**English:** Where is the post office/bank/ hotel?	**Afrikaans:** Waar is die poskantoor/bank/ hotel?
Xhosa: Hayi	**Zulu:** Cha	**Xhosa:** Iphi iposi/ ibhanki/ ihotele?	**Zulu:** Iphi iposi/ ibhange/ ihhotele?
English: How are you?	**Afrikaans:** Hoe gaan dit?		
Xhosa: Kunjani?	**Zulu:** Kunjani?		
English: Thank you	**Afrikaans:** Dankie		
Xhosa: Enkosi	**Zulu:** Ngiyabonga		
English: How much?	**Afrikaans:** Hoeveel?		
Xhosa: Yimalini?	**Zulu:** Yimalini?		

Practical guide

Arriving

By air

South African Airways has the largest number of services from the UK and Europe to Cape Town and Johannesburg, South Africa's two international airports, with flights from London Heathrow, Paris, Frankfurt, Zurich and Milan. Through its membership of the Star Alliance airline network, the airline also offers seamless connections and code-share flights to and from numerous other UK destinations via London Heathrow. From the US, SAA Flies from New York and Atlanta. Flying time from the UK is approximately 13 hours, with night flights in both directions, and the airline offers a choice of economy seating or business class flat beds. SAA also frequently has highly competitive promotional fares on offer through travel agents or its website (see below)

and has an enviable reputation for safety and punctuality.

Other airlines flying to Cape Town and Johannesburg from the UK include British Airways, Globespan (from Manchester) and Virgin Atlantic (from London Gatwick).

The main airports are:

Johannesburg International

Johannesburg airport (25 km/15 miles east of Johannesburg) serves both Johannesburg and Pretoria. Scheduled bus services link the airport with both cities, taxis are readily available and car rental companies are represented. *General enquiries. Tel: (011) 921 6262.*

Cape Town Airport

Scheduled bus service connects the airport with the city centre (about 22 km/14 miles). Taxis are available and all major car hire companies are represented.
Flight details. Tel: (021) 937 1200.

Johannesburg International Airport is modern, and compares with the best anywhere

Durban Airport
The airport is 20 km (12^1/$_2$ miles) from
the city centre. Taxis are available and
major car hire companies are
represented.
Flight details. Tel: (021) 937 1200.

Domestic airlines
SAA also operates to most
neighbouring African countries and
within South Africa, connecting Cape
Town, Johannesburg, Durban, Port
Elizabeth and Bloemfontein.

There has been a boom in low-fare
airlines in South Africa in recent years,
with half a dozen start-up airlines now
connecting Cape Town, Johannesburg,
Durban and other points. There is no
guarantee that all these airlines will
remain in business as the low-cost
airline sector is prone to mergers and
take-overs, but the main domestic
carriers at present are:
Kulula
(*Internet bookings only*):
www.kulula.com
SA Express Airlines.
Tel: (011) 978 5577, www.saexpress.co.za
1 Time
Tel: (0861) 345 345, www.1time.co.za
Nationwide Airlines.
Tel: (0861) 737 737 or (011) 344 7200.
www.nationwideairlines.co.za

International airline offices
South African Airways
Tel: (UK) 0870 747 1111
(South Africa) (011) 978 5313.
www.flysaa.com

British Airways
*Tel: (011) 441 8600 or toll free 086 001
1747.*
www.ba.com
Globespan
Tel: (00 44) 8700 541 222.
www.flyglobespan.com
Virgin Atlantic
Tel: (011) 340 3500.
www.virgin-atlantic.com
Nationwide Airlines
Tel: (0861) 737 737 or (011) 344 7200.
www.nationwideairlines.co.za

By land
South Africa has land borders with
Namibia, Botswana, Mozambique,
Swaziland and Lesotho. International
bus services connect Johannesburg with
all of these, but distances are long and
roads (with the exception of Namibia)
are poor beyond South Africa's borders.
Anyone planning to travel onward
overland to Zimbabwe should check the
current safety advice published by the
British Foreign and Commonwealth
Office or the US State Department as
the political situation within Zimbabwe
appeared increasingly volatile when this
book was last updated in 2007.

By sea
Safmarine has space for 12 passengers
in six double cabins on its 'Big White'
container ships which play between
Tilbury in the UK and Cape Town, Port
Elizabeth and Durban, with ports of
call at Algeciras and the Canary Islands.
The trip takes 14 to 16 days and costs

US$100 per person per day, including all meals.
Tel: (UK) (0238) 033 4415
(South Africa) (021) 425 2470
www.qa.safmarine.com

The RMS *St Helena* sails several times a year from the UK to Cape Town, calling at Tenerife, the islands of St Helena and Ascension, and Walvis Bay in Namibia.
Andrew Weir Shipping.
Tel: (020) 7575 6000.

Documents

Visitors must have a valid passport. Visitors from the UK, Republic of Ireland, EU, USA and Canada do not require visas. You may be required to show proof that you have access to sufficient funds to support yourself while in South Africa and you may also be asked to prove that you have a return ticket or the means to buy one.

Permitted imports
Currency

Only R5,000 in South African Reserve Bank notes can be imported, while unlimited foreign currency and traveller's cheques are allowed, provided they are declared on arrival. Foreign passport holders may not take out more foreign currency than they declared on arrival.

Drugs

Narcotics and habit-forming drugs are prohibited.

Duty free allowance

400 cigarettes, 250g (9oz) of tobacco and 50 cigars, one litre ($1^3/4$ pints) of spirits, two litres ($3^1/2$ pints) of wine, 50ml ($1^3/4$ fl oz) of perfume and 250ml (9 fl oz) of eau de toilette. Also gifts, souvenirs and all other goods to the value of R500. No person under 18 is entitled to the alcohol or tobacco allowance. Duty is levied at 20 per cent thereafter.

Camping and caravanning

Both camping and caravanning are exceptionally good value (*see 'Hotels and Accommodation' on pp166–9*). The local tourism bureau will supply information about sites.

Children

See pp156–7.

Climate

See charts and Geography and Climate on pp6–9.

Conversion tables

See p188.

Crime

See p32.

Driving
Car rental

A valid driving licence is required, as is an internationally recognised credit card. Cash is not accepted. Most companies will not rent to drivers under 21; some specify 25 as the minimum age.

Sugarbush protea, Helderberg, Western Cape

Because of South Africa's high crime rate, car rental companies in South Africa charge high insurance 'excess' levels (the amount you will have pay if your rented car is stolen, broken into or otherwise damaged). You can reduce the excess by paying an extra premium and this is recommended, as is full collision-damage-waiver insurance. All rental companies offer unlimited mileage deals.

Avis has a very extensive range of branches at airports and in city centres throughout South Africa. For those who prefer not to drive themselves, Avis also offers chauffeur-driven vehicles at selected locations. South Africa is one of the world's cheaper countries for hire car, and Avis offers a range of special deals for international visitors (you'll need your passport and airline ticket to take advantage of these).

Avis

Toll free in South Africa.
Tel: 0861 021 111.
International calls.
Tel: + 27 11 394 5433.
Central reservations. Tel: 0861 113 748.
Chauffeur drive. Tel: 0861 600 414.
www.avis.com

Budget

Toll free in South Africa.
Tel: 0861 016 622.
International calls. Tel: +27 11 398 0123.
www.budget.co.za

Europcar

Toll free in South Africa.
Tel: 0860 011 344.
www.europcar.co.za

Imperial

Toll free in South Africa.
Tel: 0861 131 000.
International calls.
Tel: +27 11 574 1100.
www.imperialcarrental.co.za

Maui

Camper van rental.
All calls. Tel: (011) 396 1445.
www.maui.co.za

Sani Van Rental

Tel: Johannesburg (011) 397 2435,
Cape Town (021) 385 0349.
www.sanirentals.co.za

Tempest/Sixt

Toll free in South Africa.

Tel: 0860 03 1666.
International calls.
Tel: +27 11 396 1080.
www.tempestcarhire.co.za

Thrifty

Toll free in South Africa.
Tel: 0861 00 211.
International calls.
Tel: +27 11 230 5201.
www.thrifty.co.za

On the road

The road network is excellent, and you
drive on the left. The speed limit in
built-up areas is 60kph (37mph), on
secondary roads 100kph (62mph) and
on freeways 120kph (74mph), unless
otherwise indicated.

Traffic laws are strictly enforced: seat
belts are compulsory; carry your driving
licence; do not drive under the influence
of alcohol. Before your departure, check
with the Automobile Association (AA)
in your country whether an
International Driving Permit is needed
to drive in South Africa.

Filling stations are plentiful on major
routes, infrequent on others. On major
routes most are open 24 hours a day
and have excellent facilities including
fast food restaurants and toilets. Most
others are open 7am–7pm. Pay for fuel
with cash – credit cards are not accepted
(some banks issue special 'petrocards').
For expert advice contact the
**Automobile Association of South
Africa,**
Tel: 0800 01 0101 (tollfree). Head office:

AA House, 66 De Korte St, Braamfontein
2001. Tel: (011) 407 1000.

Electricity

Power is delivered at 220/230 volts AC,
50Hz. Sockets accept round two-prong
plugs. Adaptors are available at stores in
the cities and bigger towns.

Embassies and consulates

South African consulates in selected
countries are listed below.

For further information go the website
of the **Department of Foreign Affairs**.
Tel: (012) 351 1000.
www.dfa.gov.za

Overseas
Australia

SA High Commission
Corner Rhodes Pl and State Circle,
Yarralumla,
Canberra, ACT 2600.
Tel: (02) 62 73 2424.
www.rsa.emb.gov.au

Canada

SA Consulate
15 Sussex Dr, Ottawa,
Ontario, K1M 1M8.
Tel: (613) 744 0330.
www.rsafrica@southafrica-canada.com

Germany

South African Embassy
Tiergartenstr 18,
10785 Berlin.
Tel: (30) 220 730.
www.suedafrika.org

United Kingdom
South African High Commission
South Africa House
Trafalgar Sq.
London WC2N5DP.
Tel: (020) 7451 7283.
info@saembassy.org

United States of America
Los Angeles:
SA Consulate
6300 Wilshire Boulevard, Suite 600,
Los Angeles, CA 90048.
Tel: (323) 651 0902.
sacgla@link2sa.com
New York:
SA Consulate General
333 East 38th St,
New York, NY 10016.
Tel: (212) 213 4880.
www.southafrica-newyork.net

South Africa
Department of Home Affairs
Subdirectorate: Visas.
Private Bag X114,
Pretoria 0001,
South Africa.
Tel. (012) 314 8911.
www.home-affairs.pwv.gov.za

Emergencies
Police emergency
Tel: 10111.

Ambulance, fire, mountain rescue, poisoning, air and sea rescue
Tel: 10177.

Child emergency
Tel: 0800 123 321.

In case of difficulties with an emergency call, Tel: 1022 and ask for the relevant service.
The Thomas Cook Worldwide Customer Promise offers free emergency assistance at any Thomas Cook Network location to travellers who have purchased their travel tickets at a Thomas Cook Network location.

Gay and lesbian
Africa Outing
Travel agency.
Tel: (021) 673 7377.
www.africaouting.com

Cape Town Pride
Website of the gay festival which takes place every February.
www.capetownpride.za

Colourful detail outside the National Gallery

Club Travel
Travel agency.
Tel: (021) 487 4218.
www.clubtravel.co.za

The Gay and Lesbian Equality Project
Tel: (011) 487 3810.
www.equality.org.za

Getting around
By air
South African Airways, Kalula.com, Nationwide and other airlines operate domestic services between Johannesburg and major centres. They also fly to selected smaller centres. Several charter and safari operators fly to out-of-the-way places. Fixed-wing aircraft and helicopters can be chartered in all major centres.

By rail
There is an efficient long-distance service connecting major cities. Trains also run to Botswana, Zimbabwe and Mozambique. Some routes involve overnight travel – services include sleeping berths, private compartments and a dining car. First- and second-class tickets must be booked at least 24 hours in advance. When booking, ask about discounts and special offers.

Overnight trains have dining cars for first- and second-class travel. Cabins are comfortably fitted out with seats that are converted to bunks at night.

Shosholoza Main Line Services is run by **Spoornet**, the national rail system

operator. Phone the central booking number in South Africa.
Tel: toll free 086 000 8888.
International calls.
Tel: +27 11 773 8920.

The Thomas Cook Overseas Timetable, published bi-monthly, gives details of many rail, bus and shipping services worldwide, and is a help when planning a rail journey to, from and around South Africa. Available in the UK from some stations, any branch of Thomas Cook, or by phoning 01733 41677; in the USA from SF Travel Publications, 3959 Electric Rd, Suite 155, Roanoke, VA 24018. Tel: 1(800) 322 3834, sales@travelbookstore.com, www.travelbookstore.com

A steam train on South Africa's railways

By bus and coach

A large number of daily coach services operate on inter-city routes, day or night. Some services also run to Mozambique, Zimbabwe, Namibia and Botswana. Try to book your ticket 24 hours in advance.

Greyhound

Customer Care (Nationwide).
Tel: (083) 915 9000 or (011) 276 8500.
www.greyhound.co.za

Intercape

Reservations and enquiries.
Tel: (021) 380 4444. www.intercape.co.za

Springbok-Atlas

Reservations and enquiries.
Tel: (011) 396 1053.
www.springbokatlas.co.za

Translux

One of the largest operators.
Reservations and enquiries.
Tel: Johannesburg (011) 774 3333,
Cape Town (021) 449 3333 and
Durban (031) 308 8111.
www.translux.co.za

The Baz Bus

Offers backpackers and budget travellers a service that takes in most of the major tourist attractions between Johannesburg, Durban and Cape Town including the Garden Route. Also to Swaziland. Flexible packages available.
Tel: (021) 439 2343.
www.bazbus.com

A typical bus stop in rural South Africa

Hitch-hiking

Although hitch-hiking is widespread, as many South Africans do not own cars, it is inadvisable for tourists. Be cautious before giving lifts or accepting them.

Health
AIDS

As everywhere, be cautious about HIV infection and take the usual precautions. AIDS is highly prevalent in African countries, and South Africa is no exception (*see box on p13*).

Drinking water

Tap water is purified and is 100 per cent safe to drink.

Hospitals and doctors

Doctors are listed in local telephone directories under 'Medical Practitioners'. Most large hospitals have efficient casualty sections open 24 hours a day.

Inoculations

Visitors from most western countries do not require inoculation certificates. It is best, however, to seek medical advice if travelling through other parts of Africa before visiting South Africa.

Insects – bites and stings

In South Africa there are a number of insects or creatures that cause bites or stings. Most are relatively minor, but African bee stings can be quite virulent. Anti-histamine cream is usually adequate to ease the pain, but medical advice may be necessary, especially if the child has an allergic reaction.

When visiting game reserves or rural areas it is a good idea to wear shoes at night, as scorpions are often out and about hunting. Some have extremely toxic venom and, should someone get stung, medical advice must be sought.

Blue-bottles, which sometimes wash up on beaches, are small floating creatures which can deliver a painful sting. Lifeguards usually offer assistance, but medical advice may be necessary.

Malaria and bilharzia precautions

Visitors to the Mpumalanga Lowveld, Limpopo, the Kruger National Park and the game reserves of KwaZulu-Natal should take anti-malaria medication as prescribed by a doctor.

It is inadvisable to swim in some rivers and lakes in the eastern and northern regions of the country, as the bilharzia parasite may be present.

Snakes

More than 130 species of snake occur in Southern Africa, but only about 14 species are considered to be dangerous enough to cause death in humans. Most snakes move out of the way of people, and it is extremely unlikely that you will get bitten. (More South Africans die after being struck by lightning than from snake bites.) In the event of a snake bite, it is important to stay calm and get medical advice as soon as possible. Try to remember the colour and size of the snake.

Sunburn

Skin cancer is one of the most common cancers among South Africans. Avoid the most intense hours of sunlight – 11am–3pm – and remember that water provides little protection against ultraviolet (UV) radiation. Always wear a hat. Sun protection measures are essential for young children. Use sunscreen with at least an SPF 15+.

For more information on skin cancer, and the rules of sunbathing, call the Cancer Association of South Africa (CANSA).
Tel: 0800 226 622.

Insurance

Medical treatment must be paid for by the patient. It is wise to take out travel insurance which covers accidents, illness or hospitalisation. Travel insurance policies can be purchased through branches of Thomas Cook and most travel agents.

Drivers' insurance can be taken out through car rental companies.
SA Tourmed sells travellers medical insurance that covers the entire Southern Africa region.
Tel: (021) 979 4419.
www.sa-tourmed.com

Maps

Excellent regional and city maps are available from South African Tourism and regional publicity associations nationwide. Most bookstores have a good range of local maps produced by Mapstudio.

Jacana Media produces some of the best maps and concise guides to the Kruger National Park.

Media

The South African Broadcasting Corporation runs more than 18 radio stations, broadcasting in 13 languages. It also broadcasts three major news and entertainment TV channels and one satellite channel. There are also a number of independent radiostations. Satellite TV with a large choice of international news and entertainment stations is widely available. Thousands of periodicals, journals, newspapers and magazines are published on a regular basis. There are a number of national daily and Sunday papers.

Anti-gun sculpture on the V&A Waterfront

Money matters
Currency
The South African currency unit is the Rand, denoted by the symbol R (international symbol ZAR). It is divided into 100 cents (c). Bank notes are issued in denominations of R200, R100, R50, R20 and R10. Coins come in 1c, 2c, 5c (being phased out), 10c, 20c, and 50c; R1, R2 and R5.

Exchange facilities
Banks may request identification when changing money. Shop around for cheaper commission rates.

Money transfers
If you need to transfer money quickly, go to any of the major banks for assistance.

Credit cards
Most businesses, tour operators, airlines, hotels and restaurants accept international credit cards including VISA, MasterCard, American Express and Diners Club. Petrol stations don't accept them.

Thomas Cook
Thomas Cook traveller's cheques free you from the hazards of carrying large amounts of cash and, in the event of loss or theft, can quickly be refunded. South African Rand cheques are recommended, though cheques in all other currencies are acceptable. Many hotels, shops and restaurants in tourist and urban areas will accept traveller's checks.

National holidays
1st January – New Year's Day
21st March – Human Rights Day
Variable – Good Friday
Variable – Easter Monday
27th April – Freedom Day
1st May – Workers' Day
16th June – Youth Day
9th August – National Women's Day
24th September – Heritage Day
16th December – Day of Reconciliation
25th December – Christmas Day
26th December – Day of Goodwill

Opening hours
Banks are open Mon–Fri 9am–3.30pm & Sat 8.30am–11am. ATMs (cash points) are situated outside most banks and are open 24 hours a day. Shops are usually open Mon–Fri 8am–5pm & Sat 8.30am–1pm. Some stores stay open all Sat & Sun.

Parks and reserves
National parks
These are run by the South African National Parks. Most parks in KwaZulu-Natal are run by Ezemvelo KZN Wildlife. The other provinces also run the smaller parks in their areas.

Entrances to parks and reserves close at sunset, but aim to arrive well before that. It is best to do thorough research before booking accommodation to ensure that your wildlife experience meets your expectations. Travel agents will be willing to help or you can visit the following websites.

SA National Parks
www.park-sa.co.za
KZN Wildlife
www.kznwildlife.com
South Africa Tourism
www.southafrica.net
Call Centre. Tel: (083) 123 2345.

Regional tourism offices will have details of smaller parks (*see regional tourism websites on p187–8*). Most travel agents and the South African Tourism website have details of private game reserves and lodges.

Pharmacies

There are numerous pharmacies nationwide and they are easy to find. Should you require medicine after hours, it is best to ask at the hotel or B&B, as very few pharmacies stay open at night. Some private hospitals have pharmacies that are sometimes open later than others.

Places of worship

Churches of every denomination, synagogues, mosques and Hindu temples are all represented in abundance. Generally, South Africa's population is religiously oriented, and religious beliefs play an important role in public affairs.

Police

The South African Police Service (SAPS) can be contacted 24 hours a day. (See listing of SA Police Service under Government Departments in local phone directories.)

Many small hotels and B&Bs may also hire the services of private security companies that respond to burglar alarms. Management will give you details if applicable.

Post

Post office hours are Mon–Fri 8.30am–4.30pm, Sat 9am–12am. Letters and parcels can also be mailed via the Postnet chain of stores, which has branches nationwide.

Prices and tax

South African prices have increased considerably over the past few years so it is worth doing some research before booking accommodation and tours. Having said that, petrol is relatively inexpensive, as are local wines and spirits.

VAT, currently at the rate of 14 per cent, is levied on most items and services, including hotel accommodation, goods, transport and tours. You can claim VAT back on goods priced higher than R250 at the airport of departure, various harbours, and customs offices. The original tax invoice, the VAT refund control sheet, your passport and the item are required. Please refer to the VAT shop at the international airport.

Public transport

Public transport in most South African cities is erratic. There are bus services in most of the bigger cities, but they tend to stick to limited routes,

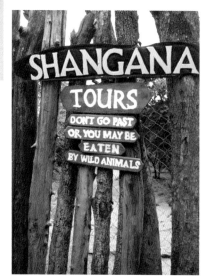

A sense of humour is essential in Africa

run infrequently and close down at night.

Minibus taxis are the most common form of public transport. The standard of driving, however, is usually poor, and the vehicles are often uncomfortable and sometimes unroadworthy.

Cape Town has a reasonable suburban and city rail service. Taxis can be arranged by hotels, restaurants or by looking in the Yellow Pages telephone directory. Ask for a quote before setting off.

Senior citizens

Facilities for senior citizens are not comprehensive. In general, expect discounts on cinema and theatre tickets and at some museums. If you feel you should be offered a pensioner's discount it's best to ask.

The Association for Retired Persons and Pensioners
Tel: (021) 531 1768.
Age in Action
Tel: (021) 426 4249.

Student and youth travel
Hostelling International South Africa (HISA)
Helps provide student cards, information about discounts and other services.
73 St Georges Mall, 3rd Floor George House. Tel: (021) 442 2251.
www.hisa.org.za

Sustainable tourism
Thomas Cook is a strong advocate of ethical and fairly traded tourism and believes that the travel experience should be as good for the places visited as it is for the people who visit them. That's why we firmly support The Travel Foundation, a charity that develops solutions to help improve and protect holiday destinations, their environment, traditions and culture. To find out what you can do to make a positive difference to the places you travel to and the people who live there, please visit *www.thetravelfoundation.org.uk*

Telephones
South African telephone call charges are expensive, and hotels add a significant charge to your call. Phone cards for public phones can be purchased in supermarkets, at post

One way to see Cape Town and other areas is by tour bus

offices and so on. Other public telephones accept coins.

Mobile phones can be rented at airports and at mobile phone stores. Most UK mobile phones will work in South Africa. South Africa has an

Pinelands police station, Cape Town

extensive mobile phone network, and renting a mobile phone is a far more reliable way of communicating than relying on public telephones.

Dialling codes

South Africa: 27
Cape Town: 021
Durban: 031
Johannesburg: 011
Pretoria: 012

Useful numbers

Directory Enquiries: 1023
International Operator (for booking or placing international calls): 0900
International Directory Enquiries: 0903

Thomas Cook

The Thomas Cook Network partner in South Africa is Rennies Travel, with branches throughout the country. Rennies offer foreign exchange,

Practical guide

Local musicians in the Cape Province

commission-free cashing of traveller's cheques and other services.

Rennies Travel Foreign Exchange
24 hours, nationwide.
Tel: toll free 0861 11 11 77.

Time
South African Standard Time throughout the year is two hours ahead of Greenwich Mean Time (Universal Standard Time), one hour ahead of Central European Winter Time, seven hours ahead of US Eastern Standard Winter Time and eight hours behind Australian Eastern Standard Time.

Tipping
A 10 per cent service charge is generally expected in restaurants, not usually included with the bill. Raise the tip to

15 per cent if you have been particularly well treated.

Leave something for hotel staff, such as the chambermaids. Taxi drivers should receive 5 per cent of the fare on top, and luggage porters R5 per bag.

Toilets
Most tourist venues, service stations and shopping centres are fairly well served by public lavatories. In nature reserves and national parks, standards of cleanliness are usually fairly high.

Tourist offices
South Africa
South Africa Tourism
Bonjala House, 90 Protea Rd,
Chiselhurston, Sandton.
Tel: (011) 895 3000.
www.southafrica.net

Overseas

Australia

South African Tourism
Level 1, 117 York St,
Sydney, NSW 2000.
PO Box Q120, QVB NSW 1230.
Tel: +61 2 9261 5000;
fax: +61 2 9261 2000.
blanche@southafricantourism.com.au

France

South African Tourism
61 Rue La Boetie,
75008 Paris.
Tel: +33 1 456 10197;
fax: +33 1 456 10196.
satourism@afriquedusud-tourisme.fr

Germany

South African Tourism
Friedensstr 6–10,

Accommodation for all tastes

Frankfurt, 60311.
Tel: +49 69 92 91 290;
fax: +49 69 28 0950.
info@southafricantourism.de

Italy

Via Mascheroni,
19 – 5 Floor,
20145 Milano.
Tel: +39 02 4391 1765;
fax: +39 02 4391 1158.
info@turismosudafricano.com

United Kingdom

South African Tourism
6 Alt Grove, London
SW19 4DZ
United Kingdom.
PO Box 49110,
Wimbledon,
London SW19 4XZ.
Tel: +44 (0) 20 8971 9364;
fax: +44 (0) 20 8944 6705.
info@uk.southafrica.net

United States Of America

South African Tourism
500 5th Ave,
20th Floor,
Suite 2040,
New York, NY 10110.
Tel: +91 212 730 2929;
fax: +91 212 764 1980.
newyork@southafrica.net

Regional Tourism offices
Eastern Cape Tourism
Tel: (0431) 701 9600.
www.etourism.co.za

Practical guide

Free State Tourism
Tel: (051) 430 8206.
www.fstourism.co.za
Gauteng Tourism
Tel: (011) 327 2000.
www.gauteng.net
KwaZulu-Natal Tourism
Tel: (031) 366 7500.
www.kzn.org
Limpopo Tourism
Tel: (015) 295 8262.
www.limpopotourism.org
Mpumalanga Tourism
Tel: (013) 752 7001.
www.mupumlanga.com
Northern Cape Tourism
Tel: (053) 832 2697.
www.northerncape.org.za
North West Tourism
Tel: (018) 386 1225.
www.tourismnorthwest.co.za
Western Cape Tourism
Tel: (021) 426 4260.
www.capetourism.org

Travellers with disabilities

For information about special needs – tours accommodating wheelchairs, services, handbooks and so on:

National Council for the Physically Disabled in South Africa
Tel: (011) 726 8040.
South African National Council for the Blind
Tel: (012) 346 1171.
South African National Council for the Deaf
Tel: (011) 482 1610.

CONVERSION TABLE

FROM	TO	MULTIPLY BY
Inches	Centimetres	2.54
Feet	Metres	0.3048
Yards	Metres	0.9144
Miles	Kilometres	1.6090
Acres	Hectares	0.4047
Gallons	Litres	4.5460
Ounces	Grams	28.35
Pounds	Grams	453.6
Pounds	Kilograms	0.4536
Tons	Tonnes	1.0160

To convert back, for example from centimetres to inches, divide by the number in the third column.

MEN'S SUITS

SA/UK	36	38	40	42	44	46	48
Rest of Europe	46	48	50	52	54	56	58
USA	36	38	40	42	44	46	48

DRESS SIZES

SA/UK	8	10	12	14	16	18
France	36	38	40	42	44	46
Italy	38	40	42	44	46	48
Rest of Europe	34	36	38	40	42	44
USA	6	8	10	12	14	16

MEN'S SHIRTS

SA/UK	14	14.5	15	15.5	16	16.5	17
Rest of Europe	36	37	38	39/40	41	42	43
USA	14	14.5	15	15.5	16	16.5	17

MEN'S SHOES

SA/UK	7	7.5	8.5	9.5	10.5	11
Rest of Europe	41	42	43	44	45	46
USA	8	8.5	9.5	10.5	11.5	12

WOMEN'S SHOES

SA/UK	4.5	5	5.5	6	6.5	7
Rest of Europe	38	38	39	39	40	41
USA	6	6.5	7	7.5	8	8.5

Index

Acknowledgements

Thomas Cook wishes to thank the photographers, picture libraries and other organisations for the loan of the photographs reproduced in this book, to whom copyright in the photographs belongs.

BIG STOCK PHOTOS/Craig Jewell 37
MIKE CADMAN 4, 5, 7, 9, 10, 11, 12, 14, 16, 17,18, 20, 30, 31, 34, 35, 36, 38, 39, 41, 42, 43a & b, 44, 45, 48, 49, 50, 51. 52, 53, 54, 55, 56, 57, 58, 59, 61, 63, 65, 66, 67b, 71, 75, 76a & b, 79, 81, 84, 87, 88, 92, 93, 94a & b, 95, 102, 103a & b, 106, 110, 112, 120, 121, 124, 128, 130a & b, 132, 133, 135, 136a & b, 137, 142, 143, 145a & b, 156, 157b, 159, 161, 164, 168, 172, 175, 177, 184
FLICKR/Thomas Sly 15, tony4carr 24, Gerard 33, Danie van der Merwe 185b
FOTOLIA/Shuva Rahim 70
ROBIN GAULDIE 21, 23, 40, 166, 181
PICTURES COLOUR LIBRARY 25, 144
TREVOR SAMSON 107, 108, 111, 125, 126, 127, 129a & b, 140, 141, 147, 148, 162, 170, 187
SOUTH AFRICAN TOURISM 19, 26, 27, 28a & b, 32, 60, 67a, 68, 69, 73, 74, 77, 80, 82, 85a & b, 86, 89, 90a & b, 91a & b, 96, 97a & b, 98, 99a & b, 100, 101, 104, 105a & b, 113, 114a & b, 115, 116, 117a & b, 118, 122, 131, 138, 139a & b, 150, 152, 153. 154, 155, 157a, 165
WIKIMEDIA COMMONS/Winfried Bruenken 29a, Thomas Schoch 29b, Andy Jou 179
WORLD PICTURES/PHOTOSHOT 1, 178, 185a, 186

Proofreading: DICK LLOYD WILLIAMS for CAMBRIDGE PUBLISHING MANAGEMENT LTD

SEND YOUR THOUGHTS TO
BOOKS@THOMASCOOK.COM

We're committed to providing the very best up-to-date information in our travel guides and constantly strive to make them as useful as they can be. You can help us to improve future editions by letting us have your feedback. If you've made a wonderful discovery on your travels that we don't already feature, if you'd like to inform us about recent changes to anything that we do include, or if you simply want to let us know your thoughts about this guidebook and how we can make it even better – we'd love to hear from you.

Send us ideas, discoveries and recommendations today and then look out for your valuable input in the next edition of this title.

Emails to the above address, or letters to Travellers Project Editor, Thomas Cook Publishing, PO Box 227, Coningsby Road, Peterborough PE3 8SB, UK.

Please don't forget to let us know which title your feedback refers to!